INTRODUCING

Romanticism

Duncan Heath and Judy Boreham

Edited by Richard Appignanesi

ICON BOOKS UK   TOTEM BOOKS USA

Published in the UK in 1999
by Icon Books Ltd., Grange Road,
Duxford, Cambridge CB2 4QF
E-mail: info@iconbooks.co.uk
www.iconbooks.co.uk

Published in the USA in 2000
by Totem Books
Inquiries to: Icon Books Ltd.,
Grange Road, Duxford,
Cambridge CB2 4QF, UK

Sold in the UK, Europe, South Africa
and Asia by Faber and Faber Ltd.,
3 Queen Square, London WC1N 3AU
or their agents

Distributed to the trade in the USA by
National Book Network Inc.,
4720 Boston Way, Lanham,
Maryland 20706

Distributed in the UK, Europe,
South Africa and Asia by
Macmillan Distribution Ltd.,
Houndmills, Basingstoke RG21 6XS

Distributed in Canada by
Penguin Books Canada,
10 Alcorn Avenue, Suite 300,
Toronto, Ontario M4V 3B2

Published in Australia in 1999
by Allen & Unwin Pty. Ltd.,
PO Box 8500, 83 Alexander Street,
Crows Nest, NSW 2065

ISBN 1 84046 009 1

Reprinted 2002

Originating editor: Richard Appignanesi

Typesetting by Wayzgoose

Printed and bound in Australia
by McPherson's Printing Group, Victoria

What is "Romanticism"?

The word "Romantic" derives from the Old French *romanz*, meaning the vernacular "romance" languages that developed from Latin – Italian, French, Spanish, Portuguese, Catalan and Provençal.

The medieval *romance* or *romaunt* came to mean a tale of chivalry written in one of these romance languages, usually in verse, and often taking the form of a **quest**.

Medieval romances are fanciful, heroic, extravagant tales.

Chivalric notions of honour, gallantry and devotion to women are predominant.

Our colloquial use of "romance" and "romantic" to describe intense **emotional experiences** can be traced back to this medieval sense of the word, and so can the 18th and 19th century concept of "Romanticism" as an **intellectual experience**, which is the subject of this book.

"Romantick"

The word "romantic" came into common usage in English in the 18th century, by which time the connotations of the medieval romance had expanded to encompass a wide-ranging taste for the picturesque and the fanciful: the cult of **sensibility** (or sentiment) of the mid-18th century. The classically-minded **Samuel Johnson** (1709–84), sceptical of the new tendency, defined "Romantick" in his *Dictionary* of 1755:

Resembling the tales or romances; wild, improbable; false; fanciful; full of wild scenery.

"Romantic" had in fact been used since the Renaissance to suggest free expression of the imagination in the arts, but mainly in a negative sense. Romantic imaginings were thought to interfere with the clarity of the art form, and so lay beyond the bounds of proper subject-matter. The emerging Romantic spirit of 18th century England was seen by some as a revival of Elizabethan literature and its "Gothic" tendencies. English Romanticism has been described as a "renaissance of the Renaissance".

Thanks to the influence of late 18th century German cultural theorists, "Romanticism" was adopted across Europe and the New World as a convenient description for distinctively **contemporary** modes of thought, losing in the process many of its negative connotations.

Johnson, a man of the 18th century Enlightenment, had defined the word in terms of its **past** . . .

But with a sense of its current debasement in fashionable excesses of sensibility.

*The age of "High Romanticism" made the word a focus for hopes of revolution and social change in the **future**. It became a **political** term.*

Instead of "improbable" notions and "false" sensibility, Romanticism came to stand for **authenticity**, **integrity** and **spontaneity**. It was seen as a positive artistic and intellectual assertion of the extremes in the human psyche, the areas of experience beyond logic and reason which could only be expressed in a direct and heartfelt way. These new concerns were seen as a valid response to the extremes of change and uncertainty which the age itself displayed.

"Romantisch"

In 1798, the German critic and philosopher **Friedrich von Schlegel** (1772–1829) used the term *romantisch* to describe contemporary forms of artistic expression, relating it particularly to what he called "progressive universal poetry".

> *A new term is needed to define qualities in the arts which have never been given such prominence before . . . the free expression of **imagination** and **association**.*

But what had happened in the forty years between Johnson and Schlegel to make such a difference in their attitudes? The Western world had been shaken by two political revolutions, in America (1776) and France (1789), and by an industrial revolution which was beginning to erode the traditionally agrarian lives of many people.

New ways of living had to be reflected in new ways of thinking. Romanticism, for want of any better word, came to stand for this new experience of the world. The true Romantic was not an over-sensitive dreamer, but a heroic figure facing head-on the painful realities of his time – a figure of **genius**.

The Problem Child of the Enlightenment

To understand Romanticism, it is necessary first to understand **the Enlightenment**. As the "problem child" of this great movement, Romanticism shows many of the characteristics of its parent, but equally some radical differences.

The Enlightenment affected most of the Western world during the late 17th and 18th centuries. It was above all a movement which sought to **emancipate** mankind, regardless of political frontiers, from the triple tyranny of despotism, bigotry and superstition. What were the weapons in this fight?

Momentous advances occurred in science, philosophy and politics. The discoveries of **Sir Isaac Newton** (1642–1727) confirmed the regular and ordered nature of the universe. The philosopher **John Locke** (1632–1704) asserted that only the information of the senses, experience and observation could provide true understanding of the external world. Scientific knowledge could banish superstition.

Universal Enlightenment

The aim of intellectuals was to *cosmopolitanize* their work and make inquiry an international activity which would shed light on the universal **collective** condition of man. The American and French Revolutions were given their intellectual basis by the common struggle for secular **humanistic** ideals which, in spite of their differences of opinion, united intellectuals across the Western world. The German philosopher Immanuel Kant was in no doubt about this . . .

*It is time to cast off man's immaturity through the action of the inquiring mind, even if the **limits** of possible knowledge are revealed in the process.*

Philosophers, satirists, scientists, artists, politicians and intellectuals attempted to banish man's dependence on received wisdom and the authority of the Church in favour of a theory of existence in which man could stand unaided at the centre of his own rational universe.

Intellectual inquiry across the Western world was marked by a spirit of unity and self-confidence. The colossal *Encyclopédie* supervised by **Denis Diderot** (1713–84), a work which attempted to bring together the accumulated wisdom of the age using the talents of its foremost intellects, was the definitive product of the Enlightenment ethos.

Rationalism (the theory that reason is the foundation of certainty in knowledge)
Materialism (the theory that nothing exists but matter, and that its movements govern consciousness and will)
Empiricism (the theory that observation and experiment are the foundation for knowledge)
Determinism (the theory that human action is not free, but determined by motives regarded as external forces acting on the will)
Utilitarianism (the theory that the moral dimension of human actions is determined by their capacity to produce happiness)

These were some of the philosophical approaches of the age. Man was *potentially* perfectible, and the universe potentially discoverable, through **the action of the intellect**.

Reason and Feeling

But it would be misleading to suppose that the Enlightenment was a coherent programme that privileged reason exclusively. The passions and "affections" were also recognized in both **personal** and **political** terms. The "Age of Sensibility" of the 18th century was as much a part of the Enlightenment as was the rigorous empiricism of Locke. This is made clear in a remark by the French *philosophe* Diderot.

> *It is only the passions, and the great passions, that can raise the soul to great things.*

The Enlightenment was diverse enough to encourage both the *reasoned* criticism of existing authorities and the appeal to human *feelings* to achieve the same fundamental aim – personal and political freedom. It was therefore seen as *rational* for feelings to be invoked, such was the emotional importance of the objective.

The English novelist of manners and society **Jane Austen** (1775–1817), a writer sensitive to both the rationalism and the emotionality of the age, dramatized the conflict in her novel *Sense and Sensibility* (1811).

Blurred Edges

Romanticism is often taken as the polar opposite of Enlightenment thinking. It is more accurate to see it as a *critique* of the excessive rationalism on which the Enlightenment came to rely. The reforming spirit of the Enlightenment had an undoubted liberating effect on Western man, intellectually and politically, and most Romantic artists and thinkers remained in uneasy sympathy with it.

The problem for us was the French Revolution.

Was it a culmination or a travesty of Enlightenment ideals?

The revolution made us into "problem children".

The boundaries between the Enlightenment and Romanticism are blurred. Both were **reforming** movements, characterized by intense seriousness of purpose. The liberation of the inner man was as much the aim of the Romantics as the Enlightenment thinkers, and they both shared a sense of the absolute concepts of truth and justice being within mankind's reach.

Romanticism is an essentially *encompassing* movement which does not exclude the rationalist aims that preceded it. Romanticism was the continuation of the Enlightenment by other means.

11

England, America and Revolution

America was already a symbol of hope for Europeans labouring under absolutist monarchs. The American Rebellion of 1775–6 signalled the first stirrings of the worldwide spirit of revolution that was to galvanize the Romantic age. It was a change conceived as fully compatible with the rationalist and commonsense principles of the Enlightenment, and was significantly less radical than the French Revolution.

The word "revolution", in the late 18th century, had not fully acquired its modern sense of destroying established order.

It was used mainly to describe the movement of the heavens.

But in a related sense, it also indicated a turning back – a movement towards a previous state.

Although the English radical thinker **Thomas Paine** (1737–1809) popularized the word with regard to the American rebellion, "revolution" was still not universally linked with the forces of radical change. The founders of American independence were not the dispossessed poor, but bourgeois or even patrician landowners in New England seeking parity with their English cousins.

The northeastern area of America founded by dissident English Puritans was effectively an extension of England, and the climate of thought at the time of the Rebellion was inspired by the great English prototypes of Enlightenment empiricism – philosophers Francis Bacon and John Locke, and scientist Isaac Newton. Empiricism, the science of observation, provided the moral and philosophical groundwork for the aspirations of the American colonists. The Declaration of Independence (1776) combines an **empirical** observation on mankind with a **moral** and **political** conclusion.

We hold these Truths to be self-evident, that all Men are created equal, that they are endowed by their Creator with certain unalienable Rights, that among these are Life, Liberty, and the Pursuit of Happiness.

The style of art and architecture which the American rebels adopted for the expression of these beliefs was the one to which the French revolutionaries would also turn in the following decade: **Neo-classicism**.

Enlightenment Neo-classicism

The movement from which Romanticism distanced itself was not the Enlightenment itself, but the style of art in which the Enlightenment ethos was embodied – Neo-classicism. This was the expression in artistic terms of the 18th century's search for the founding principles of humanity, stripping away the rotten layers of superstition to reveal universal *morally-based* truths. Neo-classicism flowered earlier in literature (from the late 17th to the early 18th centuries) than it did in art and architecture (late 18th to early 19th centuries).

Art, like the new society which rational inquiry will bring into being, must be founded on clear principles.

***Regularity of form** and **beauty of proportion**, as we see in the art of classical antiquity.*

With Enlightenment certainty, the artists of the late 18th century saw their style as a "true style" which brought timeless truths into the light of rational scrutiny. Neo-classicism was opposed to the wild embellishments of the earlier **Baroque**, and particularly the decadent **Rococo** style associated with the corrupt *ancien régime* in France.

Rococo artist **François Boucher** (1703–70), reflecting the artifice of the French court, had complained that nature was "too green and badly lit". For Neo-classical thinkers, "nature" became the yardstick by which art, philosophy, morality and politics were to be judged. Just as the Enlightenment philosopher Jean-Jacques Rousseau advocated the regeneration of humanity by starting afresh from "natural" states of existence, so Neo-classicism sought the improvement of mankind through the example of "primitive" purity of line and simple grandeur of form. The **paganism** of classical antiquity also recommended itself to the Enlightenment *philosophes* in their fight against Christian dogma.

The pagan philosophers of classical times are our models.

They are uncluttered by the dogma which has followed in their wake.

An objective, timeless "truth" was "out there" waiting to be revealed, and art, by valuing order, could show all the parts of this reality as a coherent set of relations. Classical art was admired because it was executed with the aim of imposing order onto chaos.

More Blurred Edges

Recent criticism has tended to de-simplify Neo-classicism, as it has Romanticism, and to see many trends within the movement. A good example is the archetypal Neo-classicist and founder of art history, **Johann Joachim Winckelmann** (1717–68), a crucial figure in promoting what has been called "the subjectivization of antiquity". He responded to the art of ancient Greece with a proto-Romantic passion which was unheard of in the work of previous antiquarians. By giving free rein to his sensibility in judging works of art, Winckelmann anticipated Romantic aesthetics.

One can see in ancient classical sculpture the organic forms of forests and waterfalls.

As Hugh Honour has suggested: "It is with Winckelmann that art begins to replace religion and the aesthetic experience the mystical revelation." Winckelmann inspired a peculiar hybrid of "romanticized classicism".

The Gothic Revival

Neo-classicism was opposed by another trend in 18th century northern Europe – the revival of medieval Gothic architecture and a widespread popular taste for the "Gothic" in literature. Both movements were neatly encapsulated in England by **Horace Walpole** (1717–97), who not only built the first major monument to the revival in the form of his Gothic house, Strawberry Hill (1748), but also wrote the first great "Gothic novel", *The Castle of Otranto* (1764).

One must have taste to be sensible of the beauties of Grecian architecture, one only wants passions to feel Gothic.

The adoption of the term "Gothic" signified a rather arbitrary borrowing of motifs from what was perceived as a desirable medieval and feudal way of life. This held enormous appeal for nascent Romantics. "Gothick" was initially seen as an eccentric and unfocused movement, but, like Neo-classicism, it appealed to the taste for the "primitive", and its archaic "gloomth" addressed the new interest in extremes of sensibility.

Gothic Architecture

Gothic architecture was construed as a naturalistic, "organic", Christian idiom more attuned to the traditions of northern European culture than the "pagan" classicism then in vogue. The English poet Coleridge recognized this: "A Gothic cathedral is the petrification of our religion."

Gothic was also a link with a northern European mythical past, as **J.H. Fuseli** (1741–1825), painter of the Gothic sublime and friend of William Blake, pointed out.

Romantic nationalists tended to look back to medieval life as an archetype to be imitated. British Gothic imitated a pre-Reformation Catholic past. But such nostalgia was a contradiction in Britain, since Romanticism itself sprang from essentially Protestant principles of self-determination and individual faith.

Sublime Imaginings

One unforeseen side-effect of the Enlightenment was to illuminate the unexplored recesses of the material world. Empirical scientific inquiry, which had assumed that the Divine Order of the cosmos was waiting to be discovered beneath natural systems, succeeded in demonstrating exactly how complex and impenetrable the physical world could be. The scientist **Sir Humphry Davy** (1778–1829) felt this sense of frustration. His reaction to it is essentially Romantic.

Though we can perceive, develop, and even produce by means of our instruments of experiment, an almost infinite variety of minute phaenomena, yet we are incapable of determining the general laws by which they are governed; and in attempting to define them, we are lost in obscure though sublime imaginings concerning unknown agencies.

The sense of the **sublime** (the "exalted", the "awe-inspiring") was increasingly used to bridge the gap between the limited human faculties of understanding and the unimaginable infinity of the physical universe.

Classical Tour, Romantic Journey

The "Grand Tour" had a strong formative influence on this proto-Romantic passion for the sublime. The "grand tourists" were the sons of wealthy English or north European families despatched to Italy to absorb the glories of the classical past. But to reach the home of classical civilization, they had to negotiate the Romantic wilderness of the Alps, which came to epitomize for them the landscape of sublimity. The vogue for such tourism of the sublime was satirized in Laurence Sterne's *A Sentimental Journey through France and Italy* (1768).

The poet **Thomas Gray** (1716–71) and the Gothic novelist Horace Walpole gave an early account of the sublime in their description of a trip across the Alps in 1739–41. They were actively seeking new extremes of sensation as an aesthetic experiment.

Mountains, chasms and wilderness contradicted the Enlightenment principle of a well-ordered universe established by a divine "providential clockmaker".

Terribilità for the Connoisseurs

Those who could afford to travel dictated the fashion for the mountainous sublime – what Simon Schama has called "the psychology of Gothic geology". But what awaited the tourists on the other side of the Alps? Among the many classical masterpieces, there were works by two popular proto-Romantics, Rosa and Piranesi, which echoed the tourists' recent experiences in the mountains.

The work of the Italian Baroque artist **Salvator Rosa** (1615–73) anticipated "Gothic psychology" and was enthusiastically collected in the 18th century. Rosa celebrated what he called *orrida bellezza* – "wild beauty". His work had that quality of *terribilità* (fearsomeness) which was to prove so titillating for later audiences.

*His knowledge of the **Force of Shade**, his masterly management of Horror and Distress have placed him in the very first class of Painters.*

*It is said that Rosa is himself a **bandit**!*

Sublime Ruins

The etcher **G.B. Piranesi** (1720–78) pursued the emerging taste for the sublime in his treatment of the Roman ruins, giving them a "titanic" aura that encouraged those on the Grand Tour to see classical antiquity as a source of awesome, "primitive" power as well as an example worthy of imitation in contemporary art and architecture.

Once again, the boundaries of Neo-classicism, Gothic and Romantic are blurred in the pursuit of the sublime.

The Solitary Walker

The Swiss philosopher **Jean-Jacques Rousseau** (1712–78) undermines the notion that the Enlightenment was remorselessly rationalistic. He gave 18th century thought an emotional and visionary edge which has led many to see him as *the* prototype Romantic.

Rousseau was a solitary man whose individualism went to the extreme of paranoia. Not for him the "Grand Tour" by coach – he crossed the Alps alone on foot and recorded his Romantic impressions of this in his autobiographical *Confessions* (1781–88).

I need torrents, rocks, firs, dark woods, mountains, steep roads to climb or descend, abysses beside me to make me afraid . . .

Rousseau was at the same time messianic and misanthropic. The exploration of his own inner experiences surpassed mere sensibility. He elevated the self as something pure and capable of autonomous moral choices. This exclusive individualism was the basis for his lasting contribution to Romantic thinking about the self and society.

Myself, the Model

The first page of Rousseau's *Confessions* sets out his proto-Romantic creed: "I have resolved on an enterprise which has no precedent, and which, once complete, will have no imitator. My purpose is to display to my kind a portrait in every way true to nature, and the man I shall portray will be **myself**."

> . . . *I am like no one in the whole world. I may be no better, but at least I am* ***different***.

Rousseau (like Kant later) admitted that **reason** was the "inner voice" that instructed the individual to act and so ensured freedom of choice. But he extended the Enlightenment concern with the universal to suggest that it was the **feelings** generated by the *shared condition* of existence that dictated the instructions to reason. Reason and feeling were thus combined in our actions towards each other.

That at least was the theory. In practice, man's freedom to exercise his rational choice had *misled* him out of his innocent "state of nature" into decadence and conflict.

Nature and Society

Rousseau took the illusory "state of nature" as a model for a less oppressive and unequal form of civilization. He also thought that private property was the cornerstone of a corrupt modern society. Rousseau therefore differs radically from previous "social contract" theorists such as Hobbes and Locke.

In his treatise *Émile* (1762), Rousseau set out his ideas for a new method of education in which the individual would develop without the oppression of authority, in natural surroundings which allowed close links with man's originally "innocent" state. In this respect, Rousseau followed the 18th century's obsession with the **"Noble Savage"**, an imaginary figure whose simple grandeur was supposed to throw Western society's errors and horrors into ironic perspective.

Rousseau's Influence

Rousseau was also of lasting importance in the following ways:

• He anticipated the Romantic obsession with individual subjectivity.

• His individual, subjective approach to morality encouraged Immanuel Kant to develop his ambitious reform of philosophy, which was deeply influential on Romantic thinking.

• His ecstatic visionary communion with the natural world was developed by the *Sturm und Drang* movement and paradoxically led to the Romantic dilemma of the separation of the individual from the external world, the division of subject and object.

• His ideas were adopted (or rather hijacked) by the theorists of the French Revolution. In *The Social Contract* (1762), Rousseau proposed that there was a kind of "contract" between those in power and the "general will" of the citizens. The chilling invocation of this "general will" by the French revolutionaries justified the worst excesses of the Reign of Terror.
The English Romantic essayist William Hazlitt said of Rousseau:

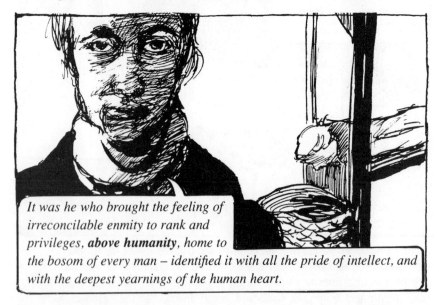

*It was he who brought the feeling of irreconcilable enmity to rank and privileges, **above humanity**, home to the bosom of every man – identified it with all the pride of intellect, and with the deepest yearnings of the human heart.*

Rousseau was therefore "revolutionary" on both personal and political levels, and central to the close association between Romanticism and revolution.

Kant and the Romantic Revolution

Like Rousseau, **Immanuel Kant** (1724–1804) was another parent of the Enlightenment's "problem child", Romanticism. Kant's **idealism** unwittingly lit the fuse for the Romantic revolution in **epistemology** – the *theory of knowledge*, which asks how we know what we know, and how reliable our basis for knowledge is.

Kant stated in his *Critique of Pure Reason* (1787) that there are **categories** (concepts such as space, time, cause, effect) inherent to the human mind which determine *a priori* (i.e. prior to our experience) how we make sense of the world.

Therefore, we are partly responsible for our own theory of knowledge, and partly the creators of our own existence.

This was a truly revolutionary concept – a "Copernican revolution" in philosophy, as Kant himself put it.

In what sense is Kant an "idealist"? In the colloquial sense of the word, classicism and Romanticism both tended to "idealize" reality. But in the strictly *philosophical* sense, idealism has a crucial role in the transition from the classical to the Romantic world-view.

What is Idealism?

Philosophical idealism is the belief that the objects of our external perceptions are "ideas" related to the contents of our minds, that what is real is essentially **psychical**.

The "idea" is therefore our basis for knowledge, in direct contrast to **materialism** which states that nothing exists but matter and its movements. Idealism derives ultimately from Plato's theory of "Ideal Forms" lying behind visible reality. As an idealist in the classical tradition of Plato, Kant conceived of an ideal world of unknowable things "as-they-are-in-themselves" (*noumena*), distinct from the material world of knowable things "as-they-appear" to our senses (*phenomena*).

I wanted to provide a critical foundation for objective knowledge.

*But if you say that we can never know the noumenal world, since we can only work within the framework of our physical senses, you set a **limit** to the possibility of knowledge.*

Man himself is that limit. And so, in Romantic thought (extrapolating from Kant), man becomes the subjective centre of knowledge. Kant's critical idealism instigated a revolution which undermined centuries of thought. We can barely understand what a terrifying prospect this was for his contemporaries.

Metaphysical Terror

Kant's intellect was essentially destructive.

Thomas de Quincey (1785–1859)

Our German philosophy is but the dream of the French Revolution. Kant is our Robespierre.

Heinrich Heine (1797–1856)

It seems that I shall become another of the many victims of folly whom Kantian philosophy has on its conscience . . . I cannot wrest myself from its chains. The idea that we can know nothing, nothing at all, about truth in this life . . . has upset me in the very sanctity of my soul. My sole and highest aim has vanished. I no longer have one. Since then, I abhor books . . .

Heinrich von Kleist (1777–1811)

Thoughts on the Sublime

Kant's idea of the sublime gave some consolation to those disturbed by the consequences of his idealism. An important precursor was **Edmund Burke** (1729–97) in *A Philosophical Enquiry into the Origin of our Ideas of the Sublime and the Beautiful* (1757). Burke contrasted the **beautiful** (in which harmony and proportion gave the beholder the sense of an ordered whole) with the **sublime** (in which the very lack of this sense evoked a productive and pleasant terror).

When danger and pain press too nearly, they are incapable of any delight, and are simply terrible; but at certain distances, and with certain modifications, they may be, and they are delightful, as we every day experience.

Obscurity, vastness and irregularity, whether in mountainous landscapes, Gothic architecture, "romantic" literature or the new structures of industrialization, gave the individual a "sublime" sense of his own limited capacity, hence his own mortality, and at the same time a vicarious *frisson* of delight in observing the source of danger from a safe distance.

Kant's *Critique of Judgement* (1790) distinguishes between the "mathematical sublime" (present in the *extent* of immense structures) and the "dynamic sublime" (in the overwhelming *force* of natural powers).

Contemplation of the sublime forces the observer to sacrifice **imagination** (which is inadequate to the task of comprehending the infinite) to **reason** (which must extend itself to contain the new sensory information). The *sense* of the sublime is therefore a *creative act* within the subject (the observer), and not something intrinsic to the sublime object in the outer world.

We readily call these objects sublime, because they discover within us a power of resistance which gives us courage to be able to measure ourselves against the seeming omnipotence of nature.

We therefore respond to the extreme sensations of the sublime by asserting the power of our own subjective reason in the face of external objective **unreason**, just as we make a moral decision out of the chaos of moral **disorder**. We make a *free* subjective judgement of value in both cases. Aesthetics and morality for Kant are both part of the same Enlightenment movement away from the mind's bondage towards a degree of autonomy.

The German Romantic Movement

German Romanticism in the late 18th century was inextricably linked with the search for **national identity**. There was no united Germany, but a group of small German-speaking states, with Prussia as the largest and most powerful. Germans had no contemporary artistic tradition which they could all share, and no cultural centre to which they could look for inspiration.

German writers and thinkers tended to resent their subservience to the French models of Neo-classicism and the Enlightenment. This became political subservience with Napoleon's invasion and occupation in 1806. Would-be nationalists could only look back to the Middle Ages and the Renaissance when Germany headed the culturally rich Holy Roman Empire. Enlightenment beliefs in the "universal" aspects of human experience made little sense in this jumble of German states.

There is no evidence of any unity here, except for our common language.

Fragmentation was the key to German experience. Any claims to a universal language of reason *separate from nationality* were met with scepticism and hostility here. **Irrationalism** and a concern with the **particular** and **local** characteristics of experience – key Romantic notions – were developed in these uniquely German conditions.

Herder on Language and History

The philosopher **Johann Gottfried von Herder** (1744–1803) began to think not only about the historical evolution of cultures, but also the problem of a specifically German culture. It was the "primitivist" influence of the Swiss/French Rousseau which decided the course of the German cultural renaissance in the decade 1770–80. Herder was a pupil of Kant, but reacted against the "universalizing" aspects of his master's thinking. He investigated **language** with the aim of showing that it was inseparable from thought, and hence central to the experience of individual cultures.

Language is essential to thought. Reflection is not something which can be carried out separately from the medium of language.

Like his predecessor, the anti-rationalist **Johann Georg Hamann** (1730–88), Herder felt that language had been underestimated in the philosophy of Kant and other Enlightenment thinkers. He saw language as the key to understanding the variety of human experience – each language was for Herder the expression of a unique culture, which could only be understood in terms of that language. This marked the beginning of a new interest in **philology** – the study of culture through texts.

Organic History

Herder was also an advocate of the "**organical form**" argument. Historical development was subject to the natural processes of birth, growth and decay. It was *not* part of some continuous linear progression, the concept of history favoured by the Enlightenment. Herder rejected the idea that there was some notional higher purpose (what postmodernists now call a "grand narrative") by which other cultures could be judged. For Herder, each culture was **specific**, formed by its own particular set of circumstances.

*Humanity develops through a series of cultural nationalisms expressed in the **Volksgeist** or "spirit of the people".*

By emphasizing that each culture should be understood in its own terms, Herder was laying the foundations of anthropology as a modern discipline. But the problem with organicist thinking is that it valorizes an abstract "totality" outside the experience of individuals. In political terms, this can be used for totalitarian ends. Herder's moderate nationalism was eventually appropriated by Nazism.

Herder extended the insights of the Italian philosopher **Giambattista Vico** (1668–1744), who anticipated the historicist approach of much Romantic philosophy. For Herder, as for the nascent nationalists who came under his influence, the Germanic past was to be valued for its tribal, folkloric, "Gothic" qualities. Medieval Gothic architecture was the symbol of this "sacred past", an "organic" architecture which embodied natural forms. Herder was not a hardline nationalist. His vision was inclusive, and, following Winckelmann's example, he recognized similar qualities in ancient Greek culture . . .

. . . spirit and body together, one single flower in bloom.

The New Science of V·I·C·O

But as I announced in 1802 . . . "Wir sind keine Griechen mehr."

The painter **Phillip Otto Runge** (1777–1810) took a harder line against the influence of classical aesthetics: he said "we are no longer Greeks". The "Germanization" of culture was under way.

Herder indulged in the characteristically Romantic activity of collecting native folksong (*Volkslieder*) as evidence of indigenous culture. He was also an ardent champion of the "folk" tradition in Homer, Shakespeare, Ossian and the Bible, and encouraged the young **Johann Wolfgang von Goethe** (1749–1832) to revitalize German literature by becoming "the German Shakespeare". Goethe responded by writing a "Shakespearean" drama, *Götz von Berlichingen* (1773).

Herder believes that Shakespeare's tragedies achieve an organic "holistic" vision of the universe in flux.

*I recognize in Shakespeare **the world**, blowing in the storm of history.*

This concept of a "storm" of historical evolution was a radical departure in Western thought. In looking to past figures such as Shakespeare, the Romantics developed a **liberal awareness** of the many varied forms which great art can take, and has taken, throughout the ages. This historical awareness of the plurality of artistic forms is one of the lasting effects of Romantic aesthetics.

Sturm und Drang

Herder's "storm of history" briefly became a reality during the turbulent decade of the 1770s. The first stirrings of Romanticism appeared at this time in the *Sturm und Drang* movement, which took its name from a play of 1775 by **Friedrich Klinger** (1752–1831) – *Wirrwarr, oder Sturm und Drang* (*Confusion, or Storm and Stress*). Klinger was an orphan and a *protégé* of Goethe, the leading light of the movement. Reaching its climax well before the French Revolution, *Sturm und Drang* was a rehearsal for the full-scale Romantic movement at the turn of the century. *Sturm und Drang* was marked by Herder's nationalism, a Rousseau-like idealism and faith in nature, scorn for artistic convention, the idea of individual experience (*Erlebnis*) as central to the creation of art – and belief in the power of **genius**.

It was known as the **Geniezeit** (*age of genius*) or even the **Goethezeit** (*age of Goethe*) . . .

Both were appropriate titles, since Goethe and his concept of genius held sway over this sudden blossoming of German culture.

Werther and the Crucible of Change

In his epistolary novel, *The Sorrows of Young Werther* (1774), Goethe created a prototype of the Romantic hero at odds with his world and doomed to destroy himself through his passionate, obsessive nature. Werther suffers from *Weltschmerz* (unease with the world) and *Ichschmerz* (unease with himself).

Werther, a semi-autobiographical figure, is an artist in love with a young woman, Charlotte, who is engaged to another man. Werther torments himself with the impossibility of his love and with his sense of isolation from the philistine society with which he is expected to conform. He seeks solace in feverish night-time excursions into the hills and forests which offer him some sense of sublime release.

I felt as if I had been made a god in that overwhelming abundance, and the glorious forms of infinite Creation moved in my soul, giving it life.

Werther's acute sensibility is divided between two states: a transcendent vision of union with the infinite, and an apocalyptic vision of change and decay.

The Dual Character

In his autobiographical *Dichtung und Wahrheit* (*Poetry and Truth*, 1811–32), Goethe described himself as someone like Werther "whose nature constantly tossed him from one extreme to the other". Werther's own *Doppelleben* (dual life) cannot be reconciled, and leads him to tumultuous self-destruction. The dual personality is a staple of the Gothic novel which was reaching the peak of its popularity at this time.

Werther's suicide saved me from committing it myself. But it did not prevent others from imitating him.

Goethe's novel took Europe by storm. Young men took to wearing blue coats and yellow breeches in honour of their hero's costume. "Wertherism" was noted as a cultural trend in England, and Napoleon read the novel seven times.

The Return to Classicism

Werther's suicide also marks the "death" of the early proto-Romantic Goethe and the decline of the *Sturm und Drang*. Goethe lost faith in the movement when he left his native Frankfurt for Weimar in 1775, where he was made prime minister by the Duke of Saxe-Weimar. Here he presided over the high point in German literature, the "Weimar classicism" of the 1780s and early 90s, which lay between *Sturm und Drang* and the Romantic revival.

My trip to Italy in 1786 opened my eyes to classical antiquity . . .

Classicism is health, Romanticism is sickness . . .

He felt that he had been "cured" of Romanticism, and those who persisted with it were held in contempt.

Versions of *Faust*

The unpublished original version of *Faust*, the *Urfaust*, also characterized Goethe's proto-Romantic phase. He published the first edition of this great poetic drama as *Faust. A Fragment* in 1790. It was continuously reworked but always acknowledged as incomplete: ". . . the whole will always remain a *fragment* . . ." Goethe was pleased with the heterogeneous character of his work in *Faust* – its "incommensurability".

In me there are two souls, alas, and their Division tears my life in two.

I have followed Shakespeare's example, showing no respect for the "unities", and mixing comedy and tragedy.

However, in his newly classical phase, Goethe suppressed some of the more fanciful elements of *Faust*'s plot, which he associated with the northern folklore tradition of "barbarian" (non-classical) art.

The Unity of Nature

Goethe also began to study science (or "natural philosophy" as it was known) as a means of proving his belief in a classical "uniform plan" for life. He was not a "scientist" in the modern sense, but relied on intuition (*Anschauung*) to achieve his insights.

*From my study of botany has come my theory of the archetypal plant – the **Urpflanze** – from which all other plants developed by metamorphosis.*

In *Zur Farbenlehre* (*Theory of Colour*, 1810) he denied the Newtonian analysis of white light into the seven colours of the prism. For Goethe, white light was **unity**. "In Nature the effects of colour – like others, such as those of magnetism and electricity – rest on a reciprocal relationship, a polarity, or whatever one may choose to call the manifestations of duality and even of plurality within a well-defined unity." It is not difficult to see a quasi-mystical, occult Romantic view of nature in Goethe's notion of "classical unity". In fact, **Rudolf Steiner** (1861–1925) based his spiritualist movement of **anthroposophy** on Goethe's "science".

Schiller – Classical or Romantic?

Johann Christoph Friedrich von Schiller (1759–1805) was Goethe's ally in the Weimar period when both struggled to reverse the excesses of *Sturm und Drang* and find a new form of classical expression. But Schiller too began his career with a *succès de scandale* in true *Sturm und Drang* style. The première of his play *Die Räuber* (*The Robbers*, 1781) caused a sensation.

The theatre was like a madhouse: rolling eyeballs, clenched fists, stamping feet, hoarse cries in the auditorium! Complete strangers fell sobbing into each other's arms, women staggered almost fainting to the door. It was a general state of dissolution, like a chaos from whose mists a new creation is breaking forth. (contemporary report)

The Robbers

Karl Moor, leader of a band of robbers, rebels against patriarchal authority and wreaks mayhem in the cause of freedom. Schiller was fascinated by the implications of Kant's idealist concept of an autonomous morality. Karl Moor understands that nothing of the old order is safe once the threshold of moral relativism has been crossed.

Two men like me would bring down the whole structure of the moral world.

Karl Moor is uneasy with the repercussions of revolutionary violence and finally repents. *The Robbers* preceded the French Revolution by eight years, but already enacted doubts about putting radical ideals into practice, a problem which dogged post-Revolution thinkers. But the leaders of the French Revolution who saw similarities between the play and their own aspirations made Schiller an honorary French citizen in 1792.

Spiel or Natural Play

Schiller was convinced that literature could change people and society
for the better. Aesthetics could be a potential force in politics. He also
believed, like Rousseau, in the power of "simplicity" to redeem mankind
from its modern condition. For Schiller, the action of modern man in
creating his own moral and imaginative universe is equivalent to the
play of children (*Spiel*) in which "reality", as decreed by reason and
science, is suspended. Art is therefore an intensely serious kind of play
which defines mankind in terms of freedom. Self-consciousness is the
enemy of Schiller's aesthetics of play.

*I now **see** myself creating . . . and
my imagination proceeds with less
freedom now it knows it has
witnesses.*

*I must reach the point
where **artifice** again
becomes **nature** . . . then
the imagination will get
its old freedom back.*

Freude or Liberated Joy

Children were the focus of a German Romantic yearning for *Ursprünglichkeit*, the archetypal state which, like that of the Noble Savage, could overcome our debased cultural adulthood. The parallel with the exhortation of Jesus in the Gospels to "become as little children" in order to achieve redemption is clear.

Children are what we were; they are what we must again become.

*I used Schiller's poem **An die Freude** (Ode to Joy) as the climax of my 9th Symphony.*

For Schiller, **joy** (*die Freude*) was the force which could unite men and women. Joy was a generosity of spirit, an expression of *emotional solidarity* with others. It was an influential idea for the Romantic age, as expressed in Beethoven's 9th Symphony. For the supporters of the French Revolution, joy was for a short while within reach.

The French Revolution

One could say that the Enlightenment became Romantic in the French Revolution of 1789. Enlightenment ideals of perfectibility through the use of reason and constitutional reform had clearly not succeeded in France, their philosophical home, where nobility, royalty and church still held sway in a manifestly unjust system. The bourgeois commoners of the "Third Estate" (i.e. neither nobility nor clergy) were forced to use direct action rather than intellectual means to achieve their ends.

There was as yet no industrial working class on any large scale which could form a revolutionary movement. The emergence of a mass proletariat was to come later with the gathering pace of capitalism in the 19th century.

The Moment of Joy

The storming of the Bastille by the "rabble" (*la canaille*, Voltaire's famous term) in 1789 marked a radical shift from the bourgeois rationalist model. It signalled the birth of an unpredictable undercurrent of violence which was to haunt the Romantic imagination. But the initial reaction of the early Romantics to this convulsion in European history was universally positive, even ecstatic. The young German philosopher G.W.F. Hegel planted a "liberty tree" with his friends in honour of the occasion, and the English poet William Wordsworth voiced the hope felt by many young intellectuals.

The Revolution was understood as a truly international and Enlightenment phenomenon. It sowed the seeds of revolutions throughout the 19th century – and beyond.

Romantic Terrorism

French Enlightenment intellectuals were aware that, unlike America, Europe's underclass of disaffected poor could be a volatile factor in any political change. Their fears proved well-founded. The rabble of urban *sans-culottes* (literally, "without breeches") became hardline Republicans in the next phase of the revolution, 1792–3, during which the essentially middle-class Jacobin* radicals had to make concessions to the labouring masses.

Then came the "Terror" of 1793–4 and its mass executions – including that of King Louis XVI – and the declaration of a Revolutionary war. The first generation of Romantics now experienced profound disenchantment with the revolutionary project. But the Jacobin leaders **Maximilien Robespierre** (1758–94) and **Louis-Antoine de Saint-Just** (1767–94) gave the Terror a Romantic justification by invoking the ideas of Rousseau.

* During the French Revolution, the Jacobins were members of a democratic republican group, identified with Robespierre, that met in the Jacobin monastery in Paris.

The Ghost of Rousseau

The Jacobin activists of the French Revolution formulated a "cult of the Supreme Being", based on Rousseau's mystical communion with the natural world, which would take the place of traditional Christian morality. The anarchic aftermath of the Revolution was in fact a nightmare version of Rousseau's wish for a reconstruction of society from the unconstrained "state of nature".

*Because we are true to nature, as Rousseau teaches, we are **incorruptibles** . . .*

It became clear that the legacy of Rousseau's proto-Romantic views was destruction and anarchy – just as Kant's ideas had become linked to a "metaphysical terror" in the realms of philosophy. As the German poet **Heinrich Heine** (1797–1856) put it: "Maximilien Robespierre was nothing but the hand of Jean-Jacques Rousseau, the bloody hand that drew from the womb of time the body whose soul Rousseau had created." The exhilarating nightmare of revolutionary chaos is a consistent undercurrent of Romanticism.

The Imperialist Revolution

The rise to absolute power of **Napoleon Buonaparte** (1769–1821), following a *coup d'état* in 1799, marked a change to authoritarian militarism. Napoleon's programme of imperialist expansionism gave proof of the final betrayal of the Enlightenment vision. But there were notable exceptions to this disillusionment. For instance, the philosopher Hegel . . .

Napoleon is the World Spirit on horseback, reaching across the world and ruling it . . .

Hegel continued to glorify Napoleon as an agent of the universal Enlightenment, now an essentially Romantic "World Soul" whose conquests banished feudalism from Europe and from Hegel's own benighted Germany.

Turning Inwards

The act of revolution, the Terror and its militarist aftermath forced artists and philosophers to acknowledge that there are elements of the illogical, irrational, uncertain, even *unknowable* in our experience of the world. The reforming zeal of many intellectuals now turned *inwards* to forge new approaches to the exploration of the "inner man".

Division, passion and violence are inescapable in the spiritual life of man.

But these are elements that purge and renew man's strength on the path to inner freedom.

The project of achieving enlightenment for mankind must be approached with a sense of the radical power of the irrational in mind.

Just as the *ancien régime*, the Revolution and even Napoleon were toppled, so too the old reliance on **systems** in thought fell away. The early Romantics began to pay attention to the implications of individual experience. The emancipation of the individual through *political* means had been a bloody failure. The realization of *personal* imaginative freedom was the only alternative.

The First English Romantics

The collection of poems published as *Lyrical Ballads* in 1798 by **William Wordsworth** (1770–1850) and **Samuel Taylor Coleridge** (1772–1834) has traditionally been seen as the birthplace of English Romanticism. It was anticipated by the publication in 1786 of *Poems, Chiefly in the Scottish Dialect*, by **Robert Burns** (1759–96), a collection devoted to the language of a distinct local culture and hence, in this sense, also Romantic.

Wordsworth's *Preface* to the second edition of *Lyrical Ballads* in 1800 contained a manifesto for the new poetry.

This is to be a French revolution carried out at the level of words.

Wordsworth admits the defeat of the actual revolution and the retreat into a *verbal* one. Just as the French Revolution had been the physical realization of the Enlightenment, so *Lyrical Ballads*, in echoing that revolution, would **reconceive** the Enlightenment project. Coleridge, a philosopher as well as a poet, was equally a product of Enlightenment traditions.

The Lyrical Ballads

The ballad form was chosen for their project to strike a chord with the "folk" traditions of popular culture. To write in the "language really used by men", abandoning the ornate diction of traditional poetry, was the enlightened and democratic aim of the collection. Poetry had a **rational** and **moral** purpose.

Poetry is the spontaneous overflow of powerful feelings . . .

*But it also requires **organic** sensibility and **deep** thought.*

The use of "real" language was, of course, as contrived as anything done in the contemporary 18th century style. *Lyrical Ballads* is an **artefact** which reflects the intellectual concerns of early Romantic bourgeois thinkers more than the condition of the common man of the late 18th century. Like Rousseau, Wordsworth saw modern man as alienated from his "natural" self and from his fellow men by industrialized urban life. Poetry written in the language of rural simplicity would heal this rift: "In that condition the passions of men are incorporated with the beautiful and permanent forms of nature . . ."

The "Lake School"

The term "Lake School" was coined in 1817, many years after the publication of *Lyrical Ballads*. It was a rather derogatory lumping together of the early Romantic poets Wordsworth, Coleridge and **Robert Southey** (1774–1843). "Lakers" was also a term used by Byron to express his distaste for Wordsworth and his milieu. Although these poets lived close to each other in the English Lake District at various times, their work and individual characters are too different to merit the term "school".

Southey's work is not Romantic in the revolutionary sense – he had no impulse for poetic innovation, and although he became Poet Laureate in 1813, he is now best remembered for his prose writings. He only moved to the Lakes because of his friendship with Coleridge, who shared his early Republican passions.

The friendship and collaboration of Wordsworth and Coleridge is central to English Romanticism. Wordsworth was "Nature's Priest", finding solace in the transcendental forms of his native landscape, but a "solemn, unsexual man" in the words of Byron. Coleridge, by contrast, was mercurial and unstable, never achieving the philosophical certainty of Wordsworth, but producing tormented and intensely personal visionary poems of the "daemonic" sublime, often aided by the use of drugs, of which "Kubla Khan" (1816) is the central example.

The essayist and opium addict **Thomas de Quincey** (1785–1859), another Lakeland resident, documented the lives of the three Lake poets, and contributed to public perception of what it meant to be in the "Lake School".

Criticism of the Lake School

There was never universal appreciation of the aims of the Lake School, even among the friends of Wordsworth and Coleridge. One such critic was **William Hazlitt** (1778–1830), whose comments in *The Lake School* (1818) show how mistrusted the early Romantics were, and how quickly their Rousseau-like "fundamentalism of the self" was noticed.

"They were for bringing poetry back to its primitive simplicity and state of nature, as [Rousseau] was for bringing society back to the savage state: so that the only thing remarkable left in the world by this change, would be the persons who had produced it. A thorough adept in this school of poetry and philanthropy is jealous of all excellence but his own . . ."

He tolerates only what he himself creates; he sympathizes only with what can enter into no competition with him, with "the bare trees and mountains bare, and grass in the green field". He sees nothing but himself and the universe.

Romantic Fakes: Ossian

Because the early Romantics set such great value on their own "inner authenticity", they were particularly susceptible to the creation of the "artificially genuine", i.e. fakes. One notorious fake was **Ossian**, a fictitious Gaelic bard fabricated by Edinburgh schoolteacher **James Macpherson** (1736–96) in 1762–3. Ossian's "folk epics" *Fingal* and *Temora* caused a sensation in Scotland, where Enlightenment patriots David Hume and Adam Smith welcomed them enthusiastically. Ossian swiftly became famous across Europe. Schiller praised his work, and Goethe made his Romantic hero Werther quote the bard at length. Napoleon too was a great fan.

Similarly, Thomas Percy's *Reliques of Ancient English Poetry* (1765), a collection of ballads of questionable authenticity, caused widespread interest in the medieval chivalric past. It inspired the poetry of Robert Burns and the popular medieval tales of **Sir Walter Scott** (1771–1832).

Thomas Chatterton (1752–70) forged medieval manuscripts in the name of Thomas Rowley, a fictitious 15th century Bristol poet. These were still being debated 100 years after Chatterton's death. Written when he was only 12 years old, the "Rowley" poems were assured enough as fakes to fool knowledgeable writers such as Horace Walpole. Chatterton's work was not a success, however, and he committed suicide at the age of 17. His lonely death, starving in a hovel, became a clichéd image of the suffering Romantic artist.

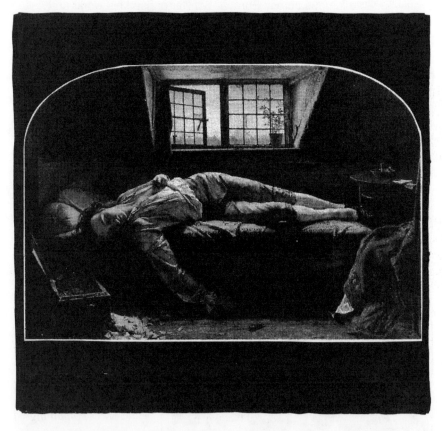

Wordsworth called him "the marvellous Boy, the sleepless Soul that perished in his pride". Coleridge wrote a "Monody" on his death. Keats, who dedicated "Endymion" to him, described him as "the purest writer in the English Language . . . 'tis genuine English idiom in English words". The French Romantic poet **Alfred de Vigny** (1797–1863) wrote a play, *Chatterton* (1835), in which he became the "poet martyr" crushed by philistine materialism. Like Ossian, the success of his forgeries says a great deal about Romantic preoccupations.

Napoleon – a "Fake Romantic"?

Napoleon remains an ambiguous figure in any discussion of Romanticism. He created an empire in the Neo-classical style, and yet he was also the Romantic adventurer, the "entrepreneur" of history, the archetype of **genius**.

As a young, victorious commander of the Revolutionary Army, he instigated a *coup* in 1799 which made him First Consul of republican France. In 1804, he proclaimed himself Emperor. Was he the "usurper" of the ideals of the French Revolution, a tyrant, or did he in fact "export" the revolution's ideals to the countries he invaded? Even those who admired him intensely were in some doubt.

*I dedicated my **Eroica** Symphony to Napoleon . . . but withdrew it when he declared himself Emperor and invaded Germany!*

I had a replica made of Napoleon's coach, in which I travelled around Italy.

There were many admirers of Napoleon the liberator, the embodiment of historical change, symbol of Romantic ideals of "titanic", "Promethean" achievement by the individual and the nation. Others such as Lord Byron, as we see, were more facetious.

The Impact of Napoleon

As a middle-class "self-made man" and opportunistic nationalist, Napoleon was a definitive product of the meritocracy of the revolution. He also extended the revolution by instituting far-reaching reforms which abolished feudalism in the states which came under his influence. He established order by centralizing local government, appointing mayors and prefects, and produced a successful national code of civil law, the *Code Napoleon*, which survived him in France, Belgium, the Rhineland and the Italian states. Some countries in Latin America adopted the Code completely as their own law.

In these respects he embodied the revolution. But he also sowed the seeds of other nationalist rebellions, directly in the countries he occupied, and indirectly by his example in other parts of the globe.

Goya: the Horrors of War

Francisco de Goya (1746–1828) was court painter to Charles IV in Madrid, and a society portraitist. But following an illness that left him deaf, he began to produce images of nightmarish intensity, beginning with *Caprices* (1793–8), a series of engravings satirizing the excesses of the established Church. Goya casts a questioning eye on the late Enlightenment world, displaying a profoundly Gothic form of Romanticism.

Imagination abandoned by reason produces impossible monsters . . .

During the occupation of Spain by the French (1808–14) under Napoleon's brother Joseph Buonaparte, Goya remained an official artist. He was also theoretically in favour of the "liberal" culture of Napoleonic France. But his strong patriotic sentiment expressed itself in two great political paintings, "The Second of May 1808" and "The Third of May 1808". His unpublished collection of etchings *The Disasters of War* (1810–14) gave full rein to his outrage. In his later years, he produced the "Black Paintings" in which there appears to be no glimmer of reason left amidst the anarchy of the universe.

Latin American Nationalism

Napoleon's presence was felt far afield in the French colony of Haiti. There, the black revolutionary **François Dominique Toussaint L'Ouverture** (1743–1803), in response to the abolition of slavery by the French Republic, established the first independent nation in Latin America. In Napoleonic style, he took the title of governor-general for life.

Toussaint brilliantly opposed Napoleon's efforts to maintain control over the colony. It was Napoleon's failure to retake Haiti that led to the sale of the other French American colonies to the USA in the Louisiana Purchase of 1803. This made the US a more powerful force in the region.

Toussaint's example was followed by **Simón Bolívar** (1783–1830), the liberator of large parts of South America from Spanish rule. Using Napoleon as his model of the soldier-statesman, and inspired also by Rousseau and the liberal ideals of the Enlightenment, Bolívar founded "Gran Colombia" (incorporating Venezuela, Colombia, Ecuador and Panama), over which he had presidential and eventually dictatorial power.

Nationalism – in opposition to his conquests – was Napoleon's furthest-reaching and most lasting export. His impact on the disunity of the German-speaking states aroused an extreme consciousness of nationhood, as we'll see.

German Romanticism: the Jena Phase

The first phase of German Romanticism was centred on the university town of Jena in Saxony between 1798 and 1804. (A second phase began in Heidelberg in 1806.) The leading *Frühromantiker* ("early Romantics") were the writer Ludwig Tieck, the critics A.W. and Friedrich Schlegel, the poet and novelist Novalis, the philosophers J.G. Fichte and Friedrich Schelling, and the theologian Friedrich Schleiermacher. **Johann Gottlieb Fichte** (1762–1814), like Herder a pupil of Kant, was the idealist philosopher who gave German nationalism its strongest voice. He marks the point of divergence from Enlightenment thinking, exemplified by Kant, into fully Romantic attitudes.

*Society is a form of **harmony** based on the "universality" of individual morality.*

*Not so! I accept Herder's view that each ethnic community has a **Volksgeist** (spirit of the people) defined in terms of its language.*

Herder's idea of culture's "organic life" became with Fichte a fixed belief in the **uniqueness** of German culture. Instead of the *harmony* of the Enlightenment project, there was now *disparity* between races and cultures. **Ethnic particularism**, a source of racism, first raises its head.

Fichte began by rejecting Kant's split between material *phenomena* (things-as-they-**appear**) and ideal *noumena* (things-as-they-**are**). Influenced by Rousseau, Fichte proposed in his *Science of Knowledge* (*Wissenschaftslehre*, 1794) that Kant's dualism could be fused in a single philosophical principle.

*The thinking "I" (or **ego**) which actively apprehends both itself (mental process) and not-itself (sense-experience) and **asserts its will on them**, is an absolute subjective reality which unites them.*

The contradiction of **thesis** (*ego*) and **antithesis** (*non-ego*) is resolved in a **synthesis** (*will*). This synthesis is the foundation for Fichte's "metaphysical nationalism". The act of the *ego* becoming aware of itself and defining itself in terms of the not-self (which it dominates) is analogous to the emerging identity of the united culture and its relation to other cultures.

The German Folk as Pure *Ego*

Fichte's notion of the individual *ego* is the central facet of experience – "I am wholly my own creation". But he was not satisfied with a world of separate selves. Identity could only come through comparison with some antithetical "other" – and Fichte wanted **group identity**. So, by some fairly murky philosophizing, he came to equate the *ego* with his "species", meaning the German people, the *Volk*. He defined the people as "pure *ego*", in the sense of "complete independence of everything which is not ourselves". The mystical paradox of freedom through submersion in the will of the many is implied here. It was to prove a potent paradox for Fascism.

The individual does not exist . . . the group alone exists.

The defeat of Prussia by Napoleon at the Battle of Jena in 1806 and its subsequent occupation was the catalyst for this development in Fichte's thought. In 1814, still under French occupation, Fichte delivered his *Speeches to the German Nation*, preaching both the "pure *ego*" of the *Volk* and the denigration of French Enlightenment culture.

A Romantic Religion of Creation

Friedrich Wilhelm von Schelling (1775–1854) developed his own form
of post-Kantian idealism in response to Fichte. Like Fichte and Hegel,
he had trained to become a Lutheran pastor (although Fichte was
suspected of atheism on the grounds of his philosophy of the *ego*).
Schelling used Romantic philosophy as a re-assertion of religious faith
against the secular anti-clerical Enlightenment. He devised an influential
philosophy of nature (*Naturphilosophie*) based on **creative intuition**. He
claimed that man could only understand his place in the universe
through an imaginative involvement with it. Confusingly, he called this
process *reason*.

*Man is able to parallel the action
of God in his own creative
insights. Man shares with nature
the urge to create, to be self-aware.
Creativity in man is faithful to the
act of creation in the divine spirit.*

*I shall take this further
in my **World as Will and
Idea** (1818) . . .*

Man was therefore linked to nature by his *willed* act of imaginative
creativity. This had a profound impact on Coleridge's idea that the
imagination was a power to reconcile man with nature. It also added to
the growing cult of the genius: the artist was a truer philosopher than
the man of pure reason. This idea was to be echoed in the philosophy
of **Arthur Schopenhauer** (1788–1860).

German Romanticism: the Berlin Phase

An early source for the propagation of the new Romantic credo was *Das Athenäum*, a literary periodical published in Berlin 1798–1800 by the brothers **August Wilhelm von Schlegel** (1767–1845) and **Friedrich von Schlegel** (1772–1829). Both were critics and accomplished translators keenly aware of the new aesthetic atmosphere in Germany following the brief *Sturm und Drang* movement. Contributors to the *Athenäum* included the theologian Friedrich Schleiermacher and the poet **Novalis** (Friedrich von Hardenberg, 1772–1801). In this periodical, Friedrich Schlegel first defined the *romantisch* in literature.

*It is the expression of incompleteness or imperfection, an embodiment of the struggle to realize the **infinite** – in contrast to the formally perfect **finite** nature of classical art.*

By endowing the commonplace with a lofty significance, the ordinary with a mysterious aspect, the familiar with the merit of the unfamiliar, the finite with the appearance of infinity, I am Romanticizing.

The Schlegels also maintained that the critic should respect the right of the creative genius to adopt his own rules for expression. These criteria were quickly accepted as the basis of a new aesthetics.

A. W. Schlegel also gave lectures in Berlin 1801–4 in which he equated "classical" with the poetry of *pagan* antiquity, and "Romantic" with modern progressive *Christian* poetry. In further lectures of 1808–9, he made the distinction between Romantic and classic as between **organic** and **mechanical** – of great importance to other thinkers, notably Coleridge who lectured on similar lines in England (1812–13).

Hegel's Aesthetics

The Schlegels' notion of the Romantic as essentially Christian and *spiritually* inspired, the classical as pagan and *physical*, relates to the *Lectures on Aesthetics* given by another Jena philosopher, **G.W.F. Hegel** (1770–1831), who moved to Berlin in 1818. Unlike his German contemporaries, Hegel remained a supporter of Napoleon, and held him in high regard for "exporting" the French Revolution into feudal Europe – even after the conquest of Jena. Hegel valued the **state** above the **nation**, which again distinguished him from other German Romantics; he deplored their conservative nationalism. Hegel remained committed to the "universal" reforming spirit of 1789.

While his hero Napoleon emulated the art of Imperial Rome with his "Empire Style", Hegel admired the sculpture of ancient Greece. For him, meaning and form are one and the same in Greek art.

The infinite is contained within the human body. So the sculpted body both expresses the infinite and gives the work of art its finite, physical boundaries.

This is opposed to the Romantic (for Hegel, everything since classical times) in which the spiritual meanings are *too abstract* for concrete realization in visual art. Romantic art was therefore art in decline.

Hegel's Dialectic

Mankind itself, however, was not in decline but progressing. Philosophy could show that historical development was drawing ever nearer to a state of **freedom** for mankind. This verdict shows the essentially Enlightenment aspect of Hegel's thinking. But the idea that freedom was to be achieved by an "organic" process shows the Romantic side of his philosophy.

Hegel's organicist concept of the **dialectic** was developed from Fichte's *thesis, antithesis* and *synthesis*.

*The dialectic is a **cumulative historical process** of surmounting conflicts, in which the **completion of all knowledge** is theoretically possible for mankind.*

Theoretically possible I could have won the battle of Waterloo

Hegel proposed that both history and logical argument proceed on dialectical lines. Conflicts in history and internal contradictions in philosophy (*thesis/antithesis*) resolve themselves through a *synthesizing* process he called *Aufhebung* (sublation). What is overcome is also preserved (or *sublated*) within the pattern of the larger totality in an organic spiral of accumulation.

Hegel's Idealism

As an antidote to Kant's destructive dualism of *phenomena* and *noumena*, Hegel (along with Fichte and Schelling) prescribed a form of idealism that would reconnect the two. This was a **monism** or "totalizing" theory which would show opposites to be aspects of the same process. For the German post-Kantian idealists, Reason was the means by which this knowledge of the Absolute (*absoluten Wissens*) could be apprehended. This is summed up in Hegel's maxim: "What is rational is actual; what is actual is rational." Mind is the only reality.

*Everything logical has its opposite or **antinomy**. For instance, proof of the existence of God is matched by proof of God's non-existence.*

*You don't go far enough. Duality also implies unity. Any state is always **linked** with its opposite or antithesis.*

You can't think of darkness, for example, without incorporating light as the antithesis which defines it, so they are inextricably linked as a unity or *synthesis*. The possibility of overcoming fixed **binary** opposites looks forward to Jacques Derrida's postmodern **deconstruction** of philosophy.

Hegel's concept of a "dialectic dynamic" behind historical development had great influence on the political theories of **Karl Marx** (1818–83). Marx converted Hegel's dialectical **theory** of human progress into a philosophy of **action** (dialectical materialism) by which the state of freedom would be *materially realized*. Hegel provided Marx with the rational basis for a "science" of revolution. Or, as Marx famously stated: "Philosophers have only *interpreted* the world in various ways; the point is to *change* it."

*My dialectic was **idealist**. The realization of freedom is possible only in **contemplation**.*

*Matter is more important in reality than consciousness. This is backed up by scientific observation. My **materialist** dialectic therefore allows the possibility of **action** for change, and not merely contemplation of it.*

Hölderlin – Romantic Philhellenist

The lyric poet **Friedrich Hölderlin** (1770–1843) is a strange and haunting figure in German Romanticism. An ardent admirer of ancient Greek culture – a **philhellenist** – he idealized and adopted the classical forms of the ode and the elegy in his poetry. His novel *Hyperion* (1797–9) also has a classical subject. But his work is at the same time an individualistic Romantic search for new ways of thinking and being.

Hölderlin conceived of a **Volksreligion** *– a pantheistic people's religion which would reunite man with his natural roots.*

In my student days, I was a close friend of Hegel and Schelling.

My passion for Hellenistic culture can be traced back to Hölderlin's influence.

Hölderlin developed an innovative, allusive style of writing which has only been fully appreciated in the 20th century climate of experimental modernism. By going back to the etymological roots of words, he invented new words which imply multiple meanings. Hölderlin's use of etymology is typically Romantic – a search for **origins**, but paradoxically focused on a classical after-world. His vision of a secret harmony between Air, Light and Earth, "three in one", is a paganized version of the Christian Trinity. Hölderlin's aim was to unify the Greek god of light **Apollo** with **Christ**.

Hölderlin was too individualistic to conform to the "Weimar classicism" of Goethe and Schiller. The poet-philosopher was, for Hölderlin, a secular priest, an isolated figure. Hölderlin suffered a breakdown in 1803 and never recovered his sanity.

Nature and the Romantics

The Romantic treatment of nature is almost always philosophical or moral. Nature and the natural life were not just the focus of Romantic disenchantment with the new urban industrial existence of the late 18th century. Nature was the mirror in which the Romantics could see the eternal powers which had made both man and the physical universe – it was no longer merely the canvas on which the classical dream of order was written. As the English landscape painter, John Constable, put it, "Painting is a science . . ."

. . . an enquiry into the laws of nature. Why should not landscape be considered as a branch of natural philosophy, of which pictures are but the experiments?

I know no Subject more ready to awake the poetical Enthusiasm, the philosophical Reflection, and the moral Sentiment, than the **Works of Nature**.

The poet **James Thomson** (1700–48) felt "a sacred terror, a severe delight" in the sublime forms of nature. His poem *The Seasons* (1726–30) was an early formative influence on both English and German Romantic nature poetry.

Nature, in revealing the hand of the Creator and the possible meaning of existence, was therefore the ground on which the greatest struggle in Romantic thinking was fought, that between **subject** and **object**.

Subject and Object

The genius who creates and yet is half-unconscious of his creation is a central paradox of Romanticism. How far does the artist control the "shaping spirit of imagination"? To what degree is it an autonomous force? Fichte's dualism of subject (me) and object (everything not-me) – the inner life of the individual and the inscrutable outer life of the world of things – leads to a tension and dialogue between the two. Committed to "subjectivity", the Romantics were fascinated by the process which led to the sense of selfhood. They were also acutely aware that their involuted search for the self would often disperse that elusive sense of identity.

In *Lines Composed a Few Miles Above Tintern Abbey* (1798), Wordsworth dramatizes the subject/object distinction in terms of the effect of natural forms on the senses.

And I have felt
. . . a sense sublime
Of something far more deeply interfused . . .

A motion and a spirit, that impels
All thinking things, all objects of all thought,
And rolls through all things . . .

. . . all the mighty world
*Of eye, and ear, – **both what they half create,***
***And what perceive** . . .*

The subject "half creates" his own universe of sensory impressions and these give him (the illusion of) an objective reality with which, because it is half his own, he can link subjectively. Sensation links man to nature – a deeply moral process.

The Egotistical Sublime

Sensation, for Wordsworth, is a kind of purified thinking, an untrammelled route into "the life of things", a "royal road" into the hidden facets of existence. Nature is the object of religious and moral veneration because it symbolizes the inner motions of our own consciousness. Wordsworth is convinced that "what we are" is the basis for our redemption – nature is our home – "The external World is fitted to the Mind".

Our everyday experience points us in the direction of the eternal. The sublime is in the human heart.

The later Romantic **John Keats** (1795–1821) was objecting to this in his description of the "wordsworthian or *egotistical sublime*".

The Uncertainty Remains

Coleridge agrees with Wordsworth that the individual consciousness contributes to its perception of the objective world. In *Dejection: an Ode* (1802), he writes:

". . . we receive but what we give,
And **in our life alone does Nature live** . . ."

But he cannot share Wordsworth's certainty that there will consistently be this healing flow between mind and nature. For Coleridge, the "shaping spirit of imagination" will *not* always apprehend the significance waiting to be discovered in the outer world.

I may not hope from outward forms to win The passion and the life, whose fountains are within.

For Coleridge, there must be an answering "joy" (a creating, synthesizing imagination) in man – without this, there can be no meaning read into the natural world. Man controls the outer world's significance completely. Coleridge sees all "joy" as centred on, and emanating from, the "pure" among mankind, those who can sustain the imaginative transaction with nature long enough to cross the boundary between the creative mind and the phenomenal universe.

Estrangement from Nature

Edward Young (1683–1765), in his influential poem *The Complaint, or Night Thoughts* (1742–5), had already allied sensation and reason as the twin faculties by which man makes his own reality.

"Our senses, as our reason, are divine
And *half create* the wondrous world they see."

By assuming that the **imagination** could provide man with a link between his subjective consciousness and the outer world of objects, the Romantic theorists and poets were in fact **estranging** the creating consciousness from the phenomenal universe to which it looked for sustenance. The more the creative imagination became established as the central feature of Romanticism, the more *self-conscious* in their work the Romantic artists became.

*By asking **how** man and nature are linked – the link is effectively broken.*

Nature and man are now more separate than ever!

Solipsism

The demands made on natural forms and on the exalting power of emotion were unsustainable. Most Romantics became aware that they could only fall back (against Schiller's advice) on the artificial world of the self-conscious creating mind. This was a form of torture, a "death in life", to poets such as Coleridge. Only through the imagination can meaning be read into nature – if there is no answering "joy" in the imagination, then the forms of nature become a meaningless backdrop.

I see, not feel, how beautiful they are!

Solipsism, the sense that *self-existence* is the only certain and verifiable part of reality, was the inevitable outcome of the internalization of Romantic aspirations. Solipsism is an exalted exclusivity which reduces all other selves and the external world to *ambivalent* status. Everything outside the self **either** has its own life **or** it is only a product of the self's awareness. This ambivalence is central to Romantic aesthetics and epistemology, most frequently expressed in the form of **Romantic irony**.

Romantic Irony

By placing human subjectivity at the centre of our experience of "reality", Kant implied that the world as it *appears* to the senses (phenomena) and the world as it truly *is* (noumena) are **distinct**. German Romantics, such as Hölderlin, Novalis and Friedrich Schlegel, developed a philosophy of Being and an aesthetic which comprehended (without necessarily bridging) this gap.

No certain conclusions can be drawn.

*The importance lies in the **act of comparison** itself.*

Placing the self in a position of meaningful tension with the mysterious objectivity of all outer phenomena . . .

This fruitful doubt was the source of Romantic irony. The uncertainty raised by the dualism of subject and object was "infinitized" to cast doubt on all fixed values and interpretations. Just as conventional irony uses what is *said* to express indirectly *what is not said*, so the "infinitized" irony of Romanticism uses the visible to allude to the invisible, the sublime, or what German philosophers called the *Nachtseite*, the "night side", of our experience.

For the German Romantic philosophers, **Socrates** (469–399 BC), as portrayed in Plato's *Dialogues*, was the model of the ironic infinitized to encompass a whole way of thinking. Socrates feigned ignorance as an oblique means of destroying his opponents' arguments. In pretending to sympathize with their point of view, he would allow the absurdity of their position to reveal itself indirectly. The "rhetorical irony" of Socrates was developed by Friedrich Schlegel, for whom irony was the basis of a new aesthetic which fused poetry with philosophy.

Philosophy is the true home of irony . . .

Irony is the form taken by the paradoxical. All that is simultaneously good and great is paradoxical.

The paradox of the Romantic imagination – bonding man to the physical world and estranging him at the same time – is an *ironic* one. So is the position of the Romantic artist or author whose work is both emotionally "real" and technically "artificial". Schlegel thought that the author should admit these paradoxes by *showing* himself in his text, revealing its artificiality through his own intrusions in the fabric of art. This has been an influential belief for much modern and postmodern aesthetics and philosophy.

World Irony

Hegel was convinced that the "irony" of Romantic expression was a self-reflexive process of increasing **abstraction** leading further and further away from his classical ideal of **sensuous beauty**. For him, Romanticism meant an "end of art" – the state in which intangible, abstract ideas have taken it over at the expense of the sensuous image. Irony for Hegel was not the positive state that it was for Schlegel. Like Schlegel, Hegel sensed "the universal irony of the world". He saw it in his dialectic of historical conflict and evolution.

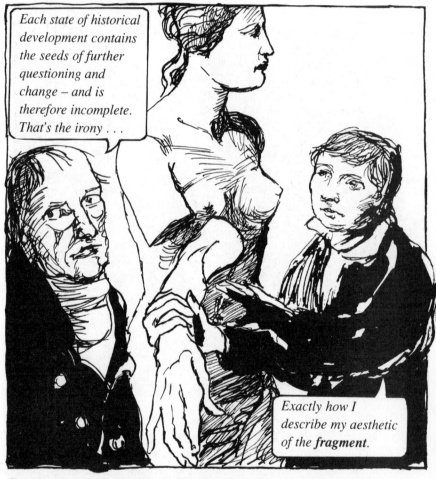

Each state of historical development contains the seeds of further questioning and change – and is therefore incomplete. That's the irony . . .

*Exactly how I describe my aesthetic of the **fragment**.*

For Hegel, though, the World Spirit or *Weltgeist* **progresses** and has the potential of a **totality** – an objective "end of history". Existence for Hegel was not the incomplete process that Schlegel describes in his view of the **fragment**.

The Romantic Fragment

The fragment – whether literary or pictorial – is the essence of ironic expression for the Romantic artist. It expresses his *awareness* of the gap between his artistic goal and the possibilities of achieving it. The Romantic fragment is also paradoxically complete and incomplete at the same time. By suggesting incompleteness, it is a more complete embodiment of the unknowability of the universe and the impossibility of rendering it artistically than a work which aims at totality. Poetry was seen as the ideal form of fragmentary expression – it was both allusive and condensed, vague and concentrated, the perfect form for a shifting, uncertain world-view.

The essential nature of the Romantic genre is that it is eternally becoming and can never be perfected.

Critical Awareness, Romantic Aesthetics

Romantic irony, as a self-conscious *critical awareness*, developed its own idiosyncratic aesthetic. A new area of thought, **aesthetics** (the philosophy of art), had emerged in the late 18th century. "Taste" was the word most often preferred to describe this new area of interest, due largely to the influence of David Hume's "Of the Standard of Taste" (1742), Edmund Burke, and Kant's *Critique of Judgement* (1790). Kant believed that aesthetic judgements are the result of "disinterested" but subjective feelings common to all people, while Hegel **historicized** art by suggesting that each historical age has a cultural *Geist* or spirit which determines its forms of art and means of interpretation.

Thinkers began to question and challenge what art *is*, what art is *for*, and how we *respond* to it. Questions of interpretation (**hermeneutics**), judgement and taste became paramount. There was a "taste for taste itself, or for essays on taste" as the satirist **Thomas Love Peacock** (1785–1866) put it. Wordsworth summed it up . . .

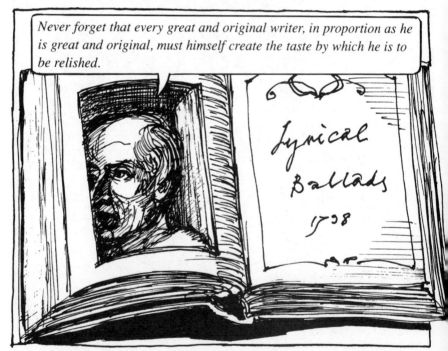

Never forget that every great and original writer, in proportion as he is great and original, must himself create the taste by which he is to be relished.

The preceding Neo-classical phase in art had tried to prescribe what "good" art should be. The Romantics were affronted by the prescriptive nature of Neo-classicism, but at the same time never tired of constructing their own explanatory systems.

The Critic and the Reader

A.W. Schlegel, in his lectures of 1808, began the process of elevating the observer or reader on a parallel with the creator of art. This looks ahead to 20th century postmodernism and Roland Barthes' famous 1968 essay, "The Death of the Author".

Coleridge developed Schlegel's ideas in his *Biographia Literaria* (1817). The Protestant theologian **Friedrich Schleiermacher** (1768–1834) lectured on critical interpretation in 1819. For him, the **individual judgement** is as important in interpreting art and literature as it is for idealist thinkers in making moral decisions. This is a radical departure in aesthetics. Every reader is now a **critic**.

Shakespeare and Romantic Critics

William Shakespeare (1564–1616) had not been highly thought of by the Neo-classical 18th century. The rehabilitation of Shakespeare's reputation was the aim of Romantic thinkers in Britain, France and Germany. He came to symbolize for them the struggle against the blind imposition of Neo-classical "rules" which shackled art. For the German Romantics, Shakespeare had an added significance.

He is our symbol of authentic, native expression . . .

. . . a model for Germans who want to be free of Neo-classical, Napoleonic France!

*For me, Shakespeare is the chief example of **negative capability**.*

John Keats's concept of "negative capability" means the ability to be receptive to all aspects of existence. This is the state in which "man is capable of being in uncertainties, mysteries, doubts, without any irritable reaching after fact and reason".

Coleridge, who pioneered the techniques of "practical criticism" of texts, was precise about his admiration for Shakespeare. Others were prone to eulogize him in more extravagant terms as a "force of nature", a fulfilment of their yearning for a symbol of organic but inscrutable complexity.

The Romantic Concept of Time

A.W. Schlegel: "Our mind has its own **ideal time**, which is no other but the consciousness of the progressive development of our beings."

In his autobiographical poem, *The Prelude* (1805), Wordsworth worked out his theory of "**spots of time**" – the joining of significant moments in the life and development of a man's mind, based on the certainty of a truth outside of time. Hegel's ideas on "modern" Romantic poetry allowed for similar events.

This theme was later developed by the philosopher **Henri Bergson** (1859–1941) in his concept of *la durée*, inner duration or **psychological time**. We experience the world not as a succession of identical, separate moments, but as a continuous progression – in the same way that we hear music *whole* rather than as a series of separate notes.

Art is a Language

Hegel's view of Romanticism as an "end of art" was not shared by other German Romantic aestheticians. They were more concerned with finding new ways of thinking about art than with delivering its death sentence. The theorist **Wilhelm Heinrich Wackenroder** (1773–98) wrote the seminal *Outpourings of the Heart of an Art-Loving Monk* (1797) in which he laid out a central German Romantic doctrine.

*Art is a language. It speaks to men through pictures, operating as a kind of **hieroglyphic** script . . .*

*The **symbol** is the hieroglyph which allows image and word to be fused.*

Nature was also a language, the language of God, able to be deciphered and read for its meaning. These languages both attested to the presence of the divine Creator. Nature was *re*-encrypted as **symbol** in the work of the German Romantic painter and theorist, **Phillip Otto Runge** (1777–1810). Runge fused the imageless concepts of his Christian faith with a piercing solidity of expression, which denied the Hegelian catastrophic prognosis of an "end of art" hastened by the introduction of abstract thinking.

Synaesthesia: the Unified Art Work

Closely related to Romanticism's "organic" aesthetic is the concept of **synaesthesia** – the fusion of separate art forms. The idea was to achieve a mystical unity of the arts, and a corresponding union of the senses, to arrive at a "super-sense" which could perceive the infinite. Runge collaborated with the poet **Ludwig Tieck** (1773–1853) and composer **Ludwig Berger** (1777–1839) to achieve a synaesthetic realization of his series of pictures, *The Times of Day*.

Our search is for a renewal of the initial inwardness of feeling felt by children.

The synaesthetic work of art would approximate the childlike ability to assimilate differing sensations into a holistic, visionary perception.

German interest in the *Gesamtkunstwerk* (unified art work) also led theorists such as Goethe and Schelling to equate architecture with music. "Architecture is frozen music", Schelling wrote. Richard Wagner later developed the *Gesamtkunstwerk* in his large-scale "music-dramas" – a fusion of myth, poetry, music and theatre.

The Inner Vision of Landscape

Another German artist who, like Runge, made innovations which allowed Romantic philosophy to thrive within art, was his contemporary **Caspar David Friedrich** (1774–1840). Friedrich's desolate symbolic landscapes examine not nature itself but the artist's own preoccupations, his ideas *about* nature; he painted *himself* in his mountainous or pastoral scenes.

The artist should not only paint what he sees before him, but also what he sees within him.

Friedrich painted not in front of nature, but in the studio, with his "bodily eye" closed and his "spiritual eye" open, transforming the experience of nature into a personal exploration. He combined landscape and interior by painting rooms with open windows looking beyond to wider spaces, often with human figures involved in the act of observation. The viewer is invited to identify with the artist's inner world, but at the same time is made aware of the boundary between the private sensibility and the world at large.

The "inner light" of individual faith was of the utmost importance to Friedrich, a committed Lutheran. Each person must be free to read a plurality of meanings into nature. Friedrich's best-known picture is almost an icon of Romanticism. "The Wanderer above the Mists" (1818) depicts the predicament of Romantic man.

The dominant figure in the foreground has attained the heights – he has achieved the heightened awareness of the Romantic visionary – and yet there is an unbridgeable gulf between him and the sublime world he observes. This is Romantic irony on a large scale.

Friedrich's most uncompromising painting, "Monk by the Sea" (1808–10), illustrates the position of man as a being estranged from the physical world by the paradox of his own self-conscious humanity. The gulf between man and nature here becomes overtly menacing. Man is like an excrescence on the blank face of nature. The German Romantic poet and critic **Clemens Brentano** (1778–1842) was unnerved by the picture, complaining that we are invited to enter the picture and identify with the human figure of the monk, but that the flat, oppressive wall of the sky and sea throws us back on ourselves.

Friedrich's deliberate reduction of perspective to a suffocating mass of impenetrable forms subverts even the Romantic idea of the sublime as ironic counterpart to the real. Some commentators have seen this painting as a precursor of abstract art.

British Romantic Landscape

With the outbreak of the Napoleonic wars and fears of invasion, the favoured Romantic landscape of the Alps became inaccessible to British seekers after the sublime. The quest turned domestic, and sensitive souls went instead to Wales, Scotland or the English Lakes.

Accidental blots on the paper can suggest a landscape of the pure imagination.

The English landscape painter **Alexander Cozens** (1717–86) published his treatise, *A New Method of Assisting the Invention in Drawing Original Compositions of Landscape* (1786), in which he set out his famous "blot system". The random blots not only reflected the irregularity of nature, the unpredictable **dynamism** of its forms, but also the imagination's own **creative** power. Landscape was an expression of the inner state.

The Shift from Classical to Picturesque

Landscape painting in Britain did not emerge as a serious genre in its own right until the late 18th and early 19th centuries. In his "Discourses" of 1769–90, the President of the Royal Academy **Sir Joshua Reynolds** (1723–92) still maintained that "history painting" was the highest form to which the modern artist could aspire, in a style modelled on classical art of the Renaissance masters Michelangelo and Raphael.

Claude Lorrain (1600–82) typified the classical ideal of landscape painting in which the "best" of nature was laid out as a harmonious whole, yet his work also appealed to the 18th century taste for the *picturesque*.

The masters of 17th century Dutch landscape painting had long been admired in Britain. But it was the **topographical paintings** of country estates or sites of archaeological curiosity, allied to the *picturesque* taste, which marked the beginnings of Romantic landscape painting. The topographers used watercolour, and this was the medium chosen by the nascent landscapists who began to explore the **effect of light**. The genre was given its most radical expression by two painters who marked a decisive break in Western painting and laid the foundations for Impressionism and the abstract art of the 20th century.

Constable: the Stay-at-Home Radical

The English landscapist **John Constable** (1776–1837) was a politically conservative Anglican countryman who radically undermined the conventions of idealized landscape art. He aimed instead for the study of the *actual* and *individual* effects of light on his own local landscapes of Suffolk and Essex. Much like Wordsworth, whom he knew, Constable used the pristine perceptions of his childhood as a kind of visionary undercurrent to the rest of his life. He was unmoved by the Romantic search for the sublime in mountainous scenery.

There is no uplifting event to justify the landscape's presence. The landscape itself is the point of the picture.

Constable saw in his native countryside an open, changing universe. His vision of harmony was of a peopled, pulsating, *worked* landscape in which every commonplace object is raised to significance by the "democratic", if transient, effects of light.

The Immediacy of Paint

Constable used small dashes of white paint to depict the effect of myriad points of light in his shifting landscapes, which he referred to as "snow". He also used *paint itself* to make the revolutionary distinction between the "immediacy" of perception and the "mediated" finished work of art. He did this by the unusual step of making full-size oil sketches of his major paintings. The pairing, as an example of Romantic irony at work, reflects the ambivalence which Constable felt towards his "final" exhibited works.

In painting "The Leaping Horse" (1825), Constable worked on the sketch and the final canvas simultaneously, unsure which should become the exhibited work.

Critics were disturbed by the roughness and fluidity of his technique. It drew attention to the painted surface itself, and made clear that this was not a leaping horse, but a *picture* of a leaping horse. The artist's sensibility is embodied in the painted surface of the picture.

Turner: the Maelstrom of Change

If Constable was passionate about the earthy domestic realities of nature, his contemporary **J.M.W. Turner** (1775–1851) was the painter who explored the sublime dramas of nature as a maelstrom of change, a light-filled abstraction. Constable's vision of a universe populated by myriad points of light is whipped up by Turner into a *storm* of light in which no single element predominates. Fire, air, water and earth are fused by the action of light. The visionary aspect of his art was reviled by many, like Hazlitt, and appreciated by others, like Constable.

Turner's work was divided between his radical abstractions and the more conformist works necessary to his survival as an artist. In spite of his Romantic individualism, he was a passionate devotee of Claude Lorrain's classical landscapes throughout his career. Turner is a good indication of the tension between self-expression and conformity which marks out many Romantics.

Turner's early masterpiece, "Snowstorm: Hannibal and his Army Crossing the Alps" (1812) is ostensibly a history painting of the type approved by the Royal Academy. Yet the narrative shrinks to the very bottom of the painting. The figures of Hannibal and his army are dwarfed by the tempest which lashes down on them.

The effect is both ironic and uplifting. The aspirations of "conquering man" set against the forces of nature seem almost comical. But the moment of the cataclysm is undeniably significant. For Turner, the maelstrom itself is the point of the picture. To paint his vision of flux and turmoil, he must use paint abstractly rather than figuratively. This technique reached its peak in his later works.

By studying outward nature intensely, Romantic landscapists paradoxically developed a more personal vision. Turner and Constable use art to reflect upon experience – and upon art itself – with ironic perspective.

Blake: the New Jerusalem

William Blake (1757–1827) worked alone, always in London, and gained little recognition in his lifetime. He was seen as eccentric, or even mad, and yet Wordsworth said of him: "There is something in the madness of this man which interests me more than the sanity of Lord Byron."

Blake devised a unique symbolic cosmology which he translated into engravings, paintings and poetry, in a synaesthetic fusion of the three media.

I must Create a System, or be enslav'd by another Mans I will not Reason and Compare: my business is to Create.

Blake was an anomalous figure in the English Romantic milieu. While his contemporaries retreated into conservative disillusionment, he never denied his revolutionary Jacobin sympathies. Blake's great theme was the apocalyptic "New Jerusalem", a conception influenced by the mysticism of **Emanuel Swedenborg** (1688–1772), and reinforced by his contact with the millennialist radicals and non-conformist religious sects in London during the late 18th century. The Bible and Milton were Blake's great literary influences. Gothic religious art and architecture were his most important visual influences.

For Blake, the **imagination** is the source of mankind's redemption, his access to the New Jerusalem, or Paradise regained on earth. Blake saw himself as a visionary and a prophet. His were not "conjured" imaginings, but clear visions. The angels he saw and spoke to were actually *present* to his eye.

I know of no other Christianity and of no other Gospel, than the liberty both of body & mind to exercise the Divine Arts of the Imagination.

The figures in his engravings combine stiff Gothic attitudes with the appearance of flayed corpses in an anatomy class, their musculature uncomfortably evident. They have the immediacy and strangeness of a vivid nightmare. These are configurations of psychological states, and their *physical* construction is as clearly shown as the workings of the *psyche* are intended to be.

Blake's psychic Romanticism is the polar opposite of Wordsworth's. He was not interested in the "Outward Creation", nature, nor in the sensations which apprehended it: "that to me . . . is hindrance & not Action it is as the Dirt upon my feet No part of Me . . ."

Fearful Symmetry

Blake's art and epic prophecies are dominated by what he sees as eternal **oppositions** and **symmetries**, much influenced by the ideas of the German mystic **Jakob Böhme** (1575–1624). Innocence and experience, love and hate, reason and imagination, heaven and hell, form a kind of dialectic which runs through Blake's private mythology. The "Mental Fight" by which imaginative Jerusalem must be regained is present in this tension between opposites. Blake is careful to allow these polarities to co-exist in his art. He does not attempt to reconcile or cancel them out, because he sees the energy released by their opposition as essential to achieving insight.

In one of his best-known poems, "The Tyger", the animal has its own unknowable, vigorous life, a "fearful symmetry" which Blake sets in symbolic contrast to the Biblical image of the docile lamb.

Did he who made the Lamb make thee

Without Contraries is no progression.

Blake also espouses a vigorous, rebellious Jesus, rejecting the conventional "Creeping Jesus" as too humble and chaste. He also values sexuality as the means whereby "the Soul Expands its wing". Blake's mysticism is a passionate and combative one.

Blake Compared

Like the German Catholic "Nazarene" group of artists (1809–29), Blake radically espoused the medieval artistic virtues of craftsmanship and moral purpose, and denied Neo-classical "Academism". But whereas the Nazarenes preferred the monastic atmosphere of the communal workshop to that of the academy, Blake was the *solitary* and self-taught artisan.

Blake held anti-industrialist sentiments and abhorred the excesses of Enlightenment reason which he thought had reduced man to a mere cog in the universal machine.

I deplore Newton's "mechanical science" for that same reason . . .

We dream of journeys through the cosmos; but is the cosmos not in us? Eternity, with its worlds of past and future, exists either within ourselves or not at all.

Blake's attitude was echoed among Romantic writers such as Novalis who saw in the Enlightenment the transformation of "the infinite, creative music of the universe into the monotonous clatter of a boundless mill . . . a mill of itself . . . a real self-grinding mill". Novalis sensed, like Blake, that exploration of the inner man was the only remedy for the modern condition.

A Utopian Project

The outcome of the French Revolution was deemed a failure by Wordsworth, Coleridge and others who felt their radical Enlightenment views of progress and liberty had been betrayed. Wordsworth continued to find solace and success in his philosophy of nature. Coleridge instead focused ever more obsessively on the functioning of his creative powers as they slipped away: "If I die, be sure to say, 'Wordsworth descended on him from Heaven; by shewing to him what true Poetry was, he made him know, that he himself was no Poet'."

One early response to disenchantment was Coleridge's scheme of "pantisocracy", a utopian project, which he developed in 1794 with the poet Robert Southey.

We'll set up a farming community on the banks of the Susquehanna river in New England . . .

. . . founded on the revolutionary principles of liberty, equality and fraternity.

Pantisocracy was an antidote to the lack of "purity" in the reforms of the French Revolution, based on the idea that small groups of individuals could attain the perfection of existence which was denied larger movements. The project failed to materialize.

Political Economy: the Dismal Science

Coleridge was seeking to renew the power of utopian *myth* in a scientific age of industrialism. Others instead embraced industrial capitalism wholeheartedly as a force for the *improvement* of mankind's condition. One such was the Scottish Enlightenment philosopher **Adam Smith** (1723–90), who founded the "dismal science" of **political economy** with his advocacy of "free enterprise" in *An Inquiry into the Nature and Causes of the Wealth of Nations* (1776).

*The pursuit of economic self-interest reveals an "invisible hand" which promotes the improvement of life for **all** levels of society.*

*The value of commodities is determined by the **amount of labour** that goes into their production.*

It is the greatest happiness of the greatest number that is the measure of right and wrong.

David Ricardo (1772–1823) concurred with Smith on free trade but also added a *labour theory of value* to "classical economics". This strictly empirical approach was further echoed in the philosophy of **Utilitarianism** developed by social theorist **Jeremy Bentham** (1748–1832). Happiness, in Bentham's system of "felicific calculus", could be *quantified* across humanity, and so moral decisions could be made on a **statistical** basis.

Owen's Social(ist) Utopianism

Coleridge's utopian myth became something of a reality with the social utopianism of **Robert Owen** (1771–1858) and his philanthropic schemes. Owen began his social experiment in 1799 by buying textile mills in New Lanark, Scotland, where he improved working conditions. By 1816, he had provided schools for child workers in his employment.

Owen advocated the replacing of **competition** (opposing the rules of classical economics) with **cooperation**.

*In 1825, I had the idea of a **self-sufficient** cooperative community, an "organic" structure in which my reforms would be more effective.*

Significantly, he chose to set up his utopia in the New World, as Coleridge and Southey had planned to do, in this case at New Harmony, Indiana. But his Village of Unity and Cooperation collapsed because its members could not agree on vital points of policy. The first experiment in British socialism was a failure, albeit an influential one. Meanwhile, in France, Saint-Simon, Fourier and others were formulating their own brand of socialist utopianism, as we'll see later.

The Second Generation of English Romantics

The fervour of the *Sturm und Drang* and nascent nationalism in Germany, and the anti-classical backlash later in France, meant that Romanticism was a much more public and political issue on the Continent than it was in Britain. The subversion of British culture by Romanticism was as radical a process as it was elsewhere, but it happened within the framework of a deeply conservative society. It was a quieter revolution.

The second generation of English Romantic poets, Shelley, Byron and Keats, were dismayed by the reactionary conservatism of their great predecessors, although they each worked self-consciously under the shadow of Wordsworth's poetic achievement, particularly his "humanized" version of the sublime.

Shelley the Infidel

Percy Bysshe Shelley (1792–1822) was fiercely politically radical, to the point of anarchism. He regarded all forms of authority as wicked, and disapproved of marriage because of the rights it denied to women. His poem *Queen Mab* (1813), for example, is anti-monarchy, anti-clerical, anti-commerce, and pro-atheism, pro-vegetarianism, pro-free love, pro-republicanism.

Known at school as "mad Shelley" and "atheist Shelley", he was expelled from Oxford in 1811 for publishing a pamphlet called *The Necessity of Atheism*. Recording his death eleven years later, the *London Courier* sneered: "Shelley, the writer of some infidel poetry, has been drowned; now he knows whether there is a God or no."

Shelley's rejection of the authority of established religion was very much the exception in the early 19th century. He was influenced in his thinking by the anarchist Enlightenment philosopher **William Godwin** (1756–1836), husband of the pioneer feminist Mary Wollstonecraft. In 1814 Shelley eloped to Italy with their fifteen-year-old daughter Mary, who, as **Mary Shelley** (1797–1851), wrote the Gothic tale *Frankenstein* (1818).

The Defence of Poetry

In his critical work, *Biographia Literaria* (1814), Coleridge paraphrased A.W. Schlegel's theory of organic form in art. He was deeply influenced by the aesthetics of the German philosophers. Coleridge's ideas on organicism were developed in turn by Shelley in *A Defence of Poetry* (1821). The act of creation for Shelley is essentially an unconscious one: the artist becomes a "maternal" channel of the work.

A great statue or picture grows under the power of the artist as a child in the mother's womb.

The only rules of art are those dictated by the inner necessity of **organic form** . . .

Shelley famously upheld the poet as the "unacknowledged legislator" of the world; poets are "mirrors of the gigantic shadows which futurity casts upon the present". He was continuing Wordsworth's "revolution in words" but from an anarchistic perspective: morality stems from individual conscience guided only by **imagination**.

Prometheus, or the Doomed Romantic Genius

Romanticism's quest for expanded powers of consciousness, in itself an over-reaching ambition, was headed for inevitable but heroic damnation. Prometheus, the Titan of Greek myth, who stole fire from the gods to benefit mankind, became the Romantic symbol of the "titanic" champion struggling against oppression for humanity's sake. Goethe's Faust is a typically Promethean figure seeking freedom, power and secret knowledge through his pact with the devil.

In punishment for stealing fire, Prometheus was chained eternally to a rock . . .

My liver was torn out by an eagle each day as it grew again.

Shelley's fully Romantic drama *Prometheus Unbound* (1820) makes the situation of his hero overtly political. He gave Prometheus the attributes of Milton's Satan in *Paradise Lost* (1667), identified as the real hero who challenges an oppressive Christian God.

Frankenstein

Mary Shelley gave the Promethean theme an added relevance to contemporary society by subtitling *Frankenstein*, "the Modern Prometheus". Frankenstein harnesses the modern "Promethean fire" of electricity to animate his creation, with disastrous results.

It was the secrets of heaven and earth that I desired to learn . . . my enquiries were directed to the metaphysical, or in its highest sense, the physical secrets of the world . . .

*. . . **Natural philosophy** is the genius that has regulated my fate.*

Satirizing the (almost exclusively male) Romantic creative ego, Mary Shelley addresses the perils of Faustian genius whose experiments acknowledge no limits but those of its own uncertain moral universe. Her novel exposes the dangerously inward-looking state of the Romantic thinker preoccupied with his own consciousness.

Electricity and the Vitalist Debate

Luigi Galvani (1737–98) discovered that a frog's legs will twitch convulsively in an electric field, and concluded that the body itself must be a source of electricity. **Alessandro Volta** (1745–1824), inventor of the electrochemical battery, rejected "galvanism" by demonstrating how a continuous electric current can be produced. These experiments with electricity provoked the "vitalist debate" of 1814–19 on the origins of life itself.

The vitalist debate was a topic of discussion between Byron, his physician Dr Polidori, Mary Shelley and her husband Percy during a stay at Lake Geneva in 1816, when *Frankenstein* was written.

Faraday and Electromagnetism

Harnessing electricity was a major scientific and technological advance of the Romantic era, and **Michael Faraday** (1791–1867) was the greatest scientist in that field. The son of a blacksmith, he became Humphry Davy's research assistant but, like his contemporary John Keats, was shunned by the establishment on account of his low-class "Cockney" background. Faraday discovered the crucial relation between electricity and magnetism.

An electric current can be produced from the mechanical motion of **magnets**.

I developed the **dynamo**, which produces electricity mechanically.

Faraday's practical "democratic" approach to science marked him out as a uniquely Romantic scientist. Shunning arcane formulae, he preferred simple language and pictures derived from experience as a means of explanation. His diagrams of magnetic fields helped to establish the modern idea of **fields** of force in place of simple mechanical force. Einstein's discoveries can be traced back to Faraday's work.

Pathological Science

While one strand of Romantic science served the cause of industrial progress, another veered towards **pathology** – the exploration of the "inner state" of man. Romantic curiosity about the irrational, the instinctive and the insane led to the development of criminology and psychiatry. Neurology grew out of the pseudo-science of phrenology. Studies of the historical development of cultures helped to found philology and anthropology.

Early Romantic "science" had sought to "pathologize" human experience by using the patterns of German *Naturphilosophie*, seeking out hidden connections between man and the universe. **Franz Mesmer** (1734–1815) and his theory of "animal magnetism" is a good example.

Animal magnetism can transmit universal forces between humans . . .

Mesmer is the beginning of hypnosis, which I also used at first – before I arrived at psychoanalysis.

The systematizing of science in the late 18th and early 19th centuries discarded these "occult" approaches. Inner experience could now be **described** and **categorized** in commonly agreed terms. Freud's work on the unconscious, instincts and "drives" grew out of the Romantic age's fascination with dreams and the hidden workings of the psyche.

Women and Romanticism

Romanticism did not follow in the path of sexual equality that Mary Shelley's mother **Mary Wollstonecraft** (1759–97) had blazed in 1792 with *A Vindication of the Rights of Woman*. She was the first feminist philosopher, an Enlightenment radical shaped by the French Revolution, who provoked an alarmist reaction. Her daughter's generation grew up burdened by a Romantic male ideology that fantasized "Woman" as an irrational creature of "feeling" and a source of domestic affection.

Inequality keeps women in a state of ignorance. Mind has no sex.

We are doomed like Frankenstein's monster, struggling for identity and yet constructed by a man . . .

Mary Shelley, like Wordsworth, carried on the revolution "at the level of words". Writing at least allowed women to compete on equal terms with men. "Gothic fiction", as an experimental form of **transgression**, permitted them to test the limits of sexuality, identity, revolution, scientific advances and decaying family bonds in abstract, fictional terms.

Keats: the Real and the Ideal

Like Wordsworth, **John Keats** (1795–1821) developed a **naturalistic** philosophy – the visible and tangible world was the measure of the sublime. But Keats had an essentially tragic vision. The imagination can only reach out to the sublime, which will always remain beyond its own mortal capacity. The ideal will always be sacrificed to the real.

This process was paralleled in Keats's own life, cut short by the encroaching fatal illness of tuberculosis. And yet, Keats's veneration for the "real" manifests itself in the sensuous richness of his poetic style.

Beauty is Truth

In his early poem, "Endymion" (1817), Keats played out this tension between the ideal and the real. Endymion's search for his Romantic ideal – Cynthia, the moon – ends when he falls for a real woman, Phoebe (Cynthia in disguise). The poem can be read as an allegory of the poet pursuing ideal beauty but constantly distracted by reality. Beauty, whether real or ideal, is the only sign of the absolute permitted to mortal man. "I am certain of nothing but the holiness of the Heart's affections and the truth of Imagination – what the imagination seizes as Beauty must be truth – whether it existed before or not."

Keats's philosophy was also **humanistic**. The primacy of the poetic imagination did not prevent him from being open to the presence of other existences. His theory of "negative capability" (see page 88) appears in his own poetry as a disinterested, non-solipsistic, imaginative openness towards all aspects of human experience.

Scenery is fine – but human nature is finer.

Keats's "negative capability" is closely linked to the concept of Romantic irony. Both are characterized by a **pluralistic** outlook. Irony emerges throughout his work in a mix of subject matter, an amalgamation of classical and medieval myths which refuses to favour either the lyrical or the tragic element. Indeed, his lyricism is an expression of his tragic conception of existence. The intense beauty of the world of things is expressible only lyrically; the unapproachability of that world can only be expressed as tragedy.

The Cockney School

Keats was subjected to vicious attacks in the press during his lifetime. He was ridiculed for belonging to the so-called "Cockney School", along with other low-born writers such as William Hazlitt and **Leigh Hunt** (1784–1859). Not only was Keats not "well-bred", but he had abandoned a respectable trade in medicine for the sake of his art. As one press critic put it: "Keats left the decent calling of pharmacy for the melancholy trade of Cockney-poetry." There is also something of upper-class snobbery in Byron's distaste for Keats's lyrical style.

*My heart aches, and a drowsy numbness pains
My sense, as though of hemlock I had drunk,
Or emptied some dull opiate to the drains . . .*

Such writing is a sort of mental masturbation – he is always frigging his imagination.

Byron also referred to him as "a tadpole of the lakes", and "Endymion" was described by *Blackwood's Magazine* as a poem of "calm, settled, imperturbable idiocy". And yet, Keats proved extremely influential on the later 19th-century Aesthetic movement which espoused "art for art's sake". He became recognized for the philosophical aspects of his work, whereas previously he was considered merely a "sensualist" writer.

Byron: the Romantic Archetype?

Asked to name the archetypal Romantic, many people would think of George Gordon, **Lord Byron** (1788–1824). His Romantic qualifications are impeccable. He led a disturbed childhood in a crumbling Gothic abbey. He had great physical beauty but was club-footed. He kept a bear in his rooms at Cambridge. His lover, Lady Caroline Lamb, called him "mad, bad, and dangerous to know". He became famous overnight at the age of 24.

What I get by my brains – I will spend on my bollocks!

His maiden speech in the House of Lords supported the Luddite frame-breakers. He had a love affair with his half-sister and was ostracized as a result. He led a nomadic life in Italy and Greece. He wrote epic yet ironic poetry. He supplied guns to Italian revolutionaries. And he died while leading Greek revolutionaries in their fight for independence against the Turks, epitomizing the liberal "philhellenist" spirit of the early 1820s.

The Sceptical Pilgrim

And yet, despite the Romantic image attached to Byron, his work has strong anti-Romantic elements. Byron deplored Romanticism, particularly that of the English "Lake School", and thought that the great tradition of English verse had ceased with the death of the Neo-classical poets Pope and Dryden. There was mutual admiration between Byron and Goethe in his mature classical phase.

Byron's sceptical stance may reflect his disillusionment with formerly radical Romantics, such as Wordsworth, and his ironic distance from the certainties of those late Enlightenment thinkers for whom the French Revolution promised everything. Exile and guilt feature strongly in his work, typified by the doomed hero of his verse-drama, *Manfred* (1817), whose sin, like Byron's, is an incestuous love for his sister.

Byron first achieved notoriety with the publication in 1812 of the first two *cantos* of *Childe Harold's Pilgrimage*, the story of a melancholy outcast and his wanderings. From the beginning, the personal myth of Byron was inseparable from the adventures of his misanthropic and defiant heroes. Byron was, like Childe Harold, the man "In deeds, not years, piercing the depths of life,/So that no wonder awaits him". To his friend Shelley, he was "the pilgrim of eternity".

the pilgrim of eternity

I have been bored ever since I was twenty.

It is a paradox that Byron's work is resolutely mock-heroic, and yet the "Byronic hero" has become the epitome of "true", heroic Romanticism. When Byron calls Childe Harold "the wandering outlaw of his own dark mind", it is hard not to identify him with his author.

Unlike Shelley, who held Neo-Platonic notions of a supersensuous reality, Byron was a sceptic and a materialist. He saw no higher reality behind the material world. His free-thinking materialism is that of the Enlightenment taken to extremes.

Don Juan – Is it Postmodern?

In his unfinished comic masterpiece, *Don Juan* (1819–24), Byron perfected his use of irony to destabilize the reader's experience of literature. He adopted an Italian verse form, popular with comic poets of the Renaissance, which lent itself to a conversational and digressive style.

Don Juan is determinedly picaresque and unfocussed in its narrative. Some critics have seen it as almost postmodern. Its diversity of subject matter – switching from personal confession to political satire, from "romantic" episodes to bawdy sexual farce – demonstrates Byron's wish to show that life cannot be contained within any system of thought.

Byron's mistress Teresa Guiccioli thought that *Don Juan* was too shocking to be published, as did the literary establishment.

The Appeal of Byronism

An outbreak of "Byronism" swept across Europe in the late 1820s, like "Wertherism" had fifty years before. What elevated Byron to arch-Romantic model was not his Neo-classical style but his political liberalism. Byron spoke for a new generation of Romantics disillusioned by the restoration of the old regimes after Napoleon's defeat but defiantly committed to revolutionary change. Byron made this clear in his criticism of Napoleon's failure, as he wrote in *Don Juan* . . .

Never had mortal Man such opportunity,
Except Napoleon, or abused it more:
You might have freed fall'n Europe from the Unity
of Tyrants, and been blest from shore to shore . . .

But he expressed only venomous contempt for Napoleon's victorious opponent, the **Duke of Wellington** (1769–1852), and all other reactionaries who shared in that victory.

And I shall be delighted to learn who,
Save you and yours, have gained by Waterloo?

The Restoration in Europe

Order was restored in Europe by the Congress of Vienna (1814–15) led by arch-conservative statesmen **Prince Metternich** (1773–1859) of Austria, **Charles de Talleyrand** (1754–1838) of France and **Viscount Castlereagh** (1769–1822), British Foreign Secretary. They counter-balanced the collapse of the Napoleonic Empire by the restoration of the pre-Napoleonic monarchies. Stability was ensured by the "Holy Alliance" of Britain, Prussia, Austria and Russia, a pan-European system of authoritarian repression with the power to intervene against revolt.

This return to the "old order" demanded constant police-state surveillance of the people. Mobilized by years of war, awakened by the collapse of feudalism, inspired by ideals of nationalism and citizenship, the "masses" posed a threat to the Restorationists.

Restoration did not succeed in stifling unrest. England is one example. From 1811–13, the framework-weavers, known as "Luddites", smashed their machines in protest against the industrial mechanization of their jobs. Luddism ended in executions. Workers' protests for parliamentary reform in Manchester resulted in the "Peterloo Massacre" of 1819. Shelley's poem "The Mask of Anarchy" (1820) was an invective response to this event.

I met Murder on the way
He had a mask like Castlereagh . . .

Threshing machines were broken and hayricks burnt (1843–44) in the Midlands and eastern counties. Desperate waves of agitation persisted in England from 1811 to 1848, the "Hungry Forties". As for the rest of Europe, armed uprisings and revolutions were chronic: 1820 in Spain, Naples, Greece; 1830s in Belgium, Poland, France; 1848 in France, Italy, Germany, the Habsburg Empire, Switzerland . . .

Revolutionary Secret Societies

The radical egalitarianism of the militant workers in England had deep roots in Millenarian religious sects and secret brotherhoods. The activists in Europe struggling against absolutist monarchies tended to organize themselves on a common model: the Masonic secret society. The stage had been set in 1796 by **Gracchus Babeuf** (1760–97), an extreme Jacobin, whose Conspiracy of Equals attempted a communist revolt which ended with him guillotined. The League of Outlaws in Germany (1834) echoed the wild ambitions of Schiller's play, *The Robbers*. This became the League of the Just in 1836, transformed under Karl Marx's leadership into the League of Communists in 1846–47.

We proclaim the need for democratic revolution and the unity of the working classes of all countries . . .

That's fine, but you'll have to drop that "secret brotherhood" nonsense.

Despite Marx's preference for a mass international workers' party, the secret society remained characteristic of revolutionary politics, indeed right up to Lenin's Bolshevik conspirators and the Russian Revolution of 1917.

Russia: the Decembrists

The Decembrists were conspirators who sparked Russia's first modern revolutionary movement in an attempt to overthrow Tsar Nicholas I in December 1825. They were mainly upper-class former army officers and Freemasons who belonged to revolutionary groups like the Union of Salvation and the Union of Welfare. Their secret societies held the appeal of a rigid hierarchical form complementary to that of the military.

They convinced three regiments of soldiers to refuse to pledge allegiance to Tsar Nicholas in the Senate Square at St Petersburg. The conspiracy failed, the leaders were hanged, the rest banished to Siberia.

Pushkin: a Russian Byron

Affiliated to the secret Union of Welfare via the literary society of the Green Lamp, the aristocratic poet **Aleksandr Pushkin** (1799–1837) was sympathetic to the Decembrists. He set out their liberal agenda in a poem, "Volnost" ("Liberty", 1817). He was temporarily exiled for his political activities, and endured a turbulent relationship with the Russian government. Pushkin was killed in a duel, defending the honour of his wife.

Freedom and peace, in substitution for happiness, I sought, and ranged unloved, and friendless, and estranged. What folly! and what retribution!
[Onegin]

The hero of Pushkin's great verse novel *Eugene Onegin* (1833) suffers from a Byronic world-weariness, a disenchanted scepticism, indulging "the bitter insights of the heart". But other figures in Pushkin's work personify an equally Byronic commitment to political liberalism.

Pushkin's one influential departure from Byron was to set the Romanticism of *Eugene Onegin* in contemporary society. This, combined with its simple but forceful language, laid the foundations for the 19th century Russian **realist** movement.

Other Russian Romantics

Pushkin's death prompted **Mikhail Lermontov** (1814–41) to produce a poem in his honour, for which he was exiled. Lermontov became Russia's leading Romantic poet. Like Pushkin, he was inspired by the "primitive" life of the wild Caucasus region, and was killed in a duel. He also produced the first Russian psychological novel, *A Hero of Our Time* (1840).

> *I also wrote Byronic poems of exile and self-destruction.*

> *Byronism for me turned into bitter comedy.*

> *We have all come from under "The Overcoat".*

Ukrainian novelist **Nikolai Gogol** (1809–52) combined realistic social protest with a strong sense of the absurd. Gogol's disgust with modern life led him to satirical realism. His story "The Overcoat" (1842) spawned a humanitarian school of writing led by **Fyodor Dostoyevsky** (1821–81).

Dostoyevsky and **Leo Tolstoy** (1828–1910) were deeply concerned with the gap between the educated élite and the mass of the "black folk" – the oppressed serfs who laboured on the vast private estates of the Russian feudal landlords. This strand of Byronic liberalism evolved over the 19th century into the "Narodnik (peasant) socialism" of the 1860s and the "scientific Marxism" of the 1880s, leading finally to Lenin and the "proletarian revolution" of 1917.

Italy: the *Carbonari*

The Italian *Carbonari* were conspirators plotting for liberal reforms against the autocratic regime of Metternich's Austria, which held Italy in a stranglehold. They were a quasi-masonic group with initiation rituals and secret signs. Their underground influence extended to France, where they had affiliations with the *Charbonnerie*, and also to Germany, spreading east during the Greek revolutionary war with Turkey in 1820.

The political aims of the various *Carbonari* "lodges" were varied . . .

The important fact was that the *Carbonari* were judged by the ruling powers to be an internationally conspiratorial threat to the *status quo*. Mainly composed of the nobility, landowners and the middle class, the *Carbonari* were essentially patriotic adversaries of the regimes imposed on Italy by the Congress of Vienna.

Crucially, the *Carbonari* laid the foundations for the nationalist "Young Italy" movement of 1831 led by republican theorist **Giuseppe Mazzini** (1805–72), and strengthened the *Risorgimento* (resurgence of national feeling), embodied in the Romantic figure of the guerrilla fighter **Giuseppe Garibaldi** (1807–82), which finally achieved unification for Italy in 1861. Mazzini and the *Risorgimento* are the definitive products of Italian Romanticism.

Young Italy was echoed in other nationalist "Youth" movements after the revolutions of 1830. Mazzini, in exile and condemned to death *in absentia*, helped to organize Young Switzerland, Young Poland, Young Germany and even Young Europe. "Young Ireland" eventually transformed itself into a notorious secret brotherhood – the Fenians or Irish Republican Army (IRA).

The poet and novelist **Ugo Foscolo** (1778–1827) was a key figure of Italian Romanticism. His ambivalent attitude to Napoleon's imperialism is indicative of the dilemma faced by many Romantics. Foscolo wrote an ode "To Bonaparte the Liberator" in 1797, but was immediately disenchanted when Napoleon handed Italian Venetia to Austria. Foscolo nevertheless fought on the French side against the Russian and Austrian invaders in 1799.

My nationalist feelings remained strong and I continued to satirize Napoleon's excesses.

During the era of Metternich he was forced into exile for his patriotic views. Foscolo's novel *Le ultime lettere di Jacopo Ortis* ("The Last Letters of Jacopo Ortis", 1802), the first modern Italian novel, dramatized the political situation in Italy at the turn of the century. Influenced by Goethe's *Werther*, Foscolo made his hero choose suicide after the betrayal of Venetia. A later but high point of Romanticism is the novel *The Betrothed* (1827) by **Alessandro Manzoni** (1785–1873).

Opera: Public Romanticism

The Italian traditions of *opera* and *bel canto* (beautiful singing) are prime examples of the Romantic form. Opera's portrayal of extravagant emotion and its focus on **human** rather than **divine** concerns make it central to the Romantic spirit. The fact that opera had "escaped" over time from the private world of the aristocratic court to the public world of mass entertainment gives it particular relevance to Romantic aspirations of freedom.

In appealing to passionate and often nationalistic feelings, opera could have direct political consequences. Beethoven's *Fidelio* (1805) set the precedent with its nationalist subtext. The première in Brussels of Daniel Auber's *La muette de Portici* (1830) actually sparked off the Belgian revolution against the Dutch. The early operas of **Giuseppe Verdi** (1813–1901) were taken as expressions of Italian nationalism. There were riotous scenes during the production in Milan of his opera *Nabucco* (1842), and the chorus "Va, pensiero" became a rallying cry for Italian resistance to Austrian occupation. Even Verdi's name became symbolic for the patriotic cause, used as an acronym for "**V**ittorio **E**manuele, **R**e **D**'Italia" ("Victor Emanuel, King of Italy").

Other major 19th century Italian operatic composers, **Gioacchino Rossini** (1792–1868), **Vincenzo Bellini** (1801–35) and **Gaetano Donizetti** (1797–1848) also contributed to the popularization of the form.

Opera – a unique combination of drama, instrumental music, sung poetry, dance, painting and architectural design – appealed to the Romantic interest in **synaesthesia** (see page 91). The *libretto* (text) of the opera increasingly adapted existing Romantic poems, novels and plays in a cross-fertilization of genres.

*I made Pushkin's play **Boris Godunov** into a masterpiece of Russian opera.*
M.P. Mussorgsky (1839–81)

*Ah, but I started it all with my heroic opera **William Tell**.*
G. Rossini (1792–1868)

*No! I did with my German fairytale opera, **Der Freischütz** (1821).*
Carl Maria von Weber (1786–1826)

None of you can match my operatic interpretations of Shakespeare.
G. Verdi (1813–1901)

The popular "folk" elements found in Shakespeare and Sir Walter Scott were transformed into such operas as Verdi's *Macbeth* (1847), *Otello* (1887) and *Falstaff* (1893) and Donizetti's *Lucia di Lammermoor* (1835). History and legend also provided inspiration for Romantic opera, for example, Rossini's *William Tell* (1829) which adapted Schiller's play of 1804 about the Swiss folk hero's triumph over oppression.

The Age of the Virtuoso

Music was one of the most distinctively "Romantic" forms of sublime expression. The artist could speak to the listener without the physical intermediary of the written word, painted surface or sculpted material. As the Victorian critic and aesthete **Walter Pater** (1839–94) said: "All art constantly aspires towards the condition of music."

The concept of the *genius* in the arts and in philosophy extended equally to music. The Romantic musical genius was a **virtuoso**, exemplified by the violinist **Niccolò Paganini** (1782–1840). Paganini wrote the music for his own performances, much of it so difficult that it was suspected that he had, like Faust, made a pact with the devil.

The 19th century virtuoso no longer, as in previous centuries, relied on aristocratic or institutional patronage. He depended on a *paying* audience of regular concert-goers – a manifestation of the new forms of urban mass entertainment.

Berlioz – Autobiography in Music

Solo "studies" or *études* specially written to exhibit the performer's genius were produced in large numbers during the period – for instance, by the virtuoso pianist composers **Franz Liszt** (1811–86) and **Frédéric Chopin** (1810–49). But perhaps the apotheosis of Romanticism in music is the French composer **Hector Berlioz** (1803–69), who, like the painter Delacroix, represents the "titanic" aspect of French Romanticism. His music is grand scale and **programmatic*** in its literary borrowings (e.g. Byron's *Childe Harold* and Goethe's *Faust*). It is also **autobiographical** music.

My life and work were transformed by a performance of **Hamlet** *in Paris in 1830.*

Berlioz became fascinated with Shakespeare, and obsessed with the Irish actress Harriet Smithson who played Ophelia and later became his wife. His *Symphonie fantastique* (1830) is an autobiographical drama of this sexual obsession, inspired also by de Quincey's *Confessions of an English Opium Eater*. In it, Berlioz invented the *idée fixe*, a recurring musical motif that binds the piece together – an influence on the *Leitmotiv* of Wagner's music-dramas.

*In "programme music", the composition is driven by an external idea: usually an image, poem, legend or story. Sometimes the "programme" behind the music was so important that composers would distribute notes and a plot synopsis among the audience.

Classical or Romantic?

The change from classical to Romantic was as imprecise in music as it was in the other arts. The key transitional figure **Ludwig van Beethoven** (1770–1827) was himself marked by both tendencies. In later life, he adopted the Romantic position of the self-driven creative artist, disdainful of patronage and composing according to his own will and talent. His work remains resolutely classical, although he injected the expressive "colour" of Romanticism into his instrumentation.

Romantic Song

The folk song or *Lied* in Germany allowed scope for personal, local and national feelings. **Franz Schubert** (1797–1828) set over 600 *Lieder* to music, which included the lyrical poems of Goethe, Schiller and other German Romantics. His cycles of *Lieder* were intended to be performed as complete poetic artworks, notably *Die Schöne Mullerin* ("Fair Maid of the Mill", 1823) and *Winterreise* ("The Winter's Journey", 1827), a musical counterpart to Friedrich's "wanderer" paintings.

These are my miniature operas.

Romantic themes from Shakespeare, Ossian, the landscapes of Scotland and Italy shaped the music of **Felix Mendelssohn** (1809–47), Queen Victoria's favourite composer. He also championed a revival of **J.S. Bach** (1685–1750). **Robert Schumann** (1810–56) in his songs, piano and orchestral pieces, forecasts a post-Romantic development.

Wagner: Unified Art Work, Unified Germany

At the opposite end of the scale to the intimate *Lieder* are the "titanic" virtuoso musical dramas of **Richard Wagner** (1813–83). Myth and drama, music and grandiose theatrical design are fused in a *Gesamtkunstwerk* (unified art work). Wagner was first inspired to produce his "music-dramas" by Beethoven's 9th Symphony, which combined orchestral music with sung poetry.

Wagner's musical genius cannot be separated from his ardent nationalism, in the mould of J.G. Fichte. Wagner was a nostalgic medievalist, an anti-bourgeois "Young German" libertarian, and virulently anti-Semitic.

I was also an active radical, taking part in the Dresden uprising of 1849.

*I had the manuscript of Wagner's opera **Rienzi** in my Berlin bunker . . .*

As Europe exploded into revolution again in 1848, Wagner was busy writing essays which diagnosed the problems of the age (he attributed most of them to Jewish bourgeois capitalism). Like the hero of his opera *Rienzi* (1840), Wagner saw himself as the purifier of a degenerate state. In the 1930s and 40s, German National Socialism appropriated Wagner's form of Romantic nationalism as a cultural justification for its own racialist "purifying" activities.

French Romanticism

Although Romanticism came late to France, one of the earliest proponents of the new movement was the French literary commentator, **Madame de Staël** (1766–1817), who continued the Enlightenment *salon* tradition of female intellectual leadership, disseminating Romantic views throughout Europe in the early 19th century. The distinction which Friedrich Schlegel had made between the "Romantic" idiom of the modern world and that of "classical" antiquity was given a wider audience by de Staël, who published *De L' Allemagne*, a review of German cultural trends, in 1813.

*Mme de Staël made the British public familiar with the habit of distinguishing the productions of antiquity by the appellation **classic**, those of modern times by that of **romantic**.*

Earlier, in 1800, de Staël had anticipated the Romantic concerns of nationhood and individuality in *De la littérature*, in which she put forward the still radical notion that literature should reflect the spirit of the time and place in which it was conceived – the *Zeitgeist*. De Staël made the breakthrough of seeing literature as a product of environment and social institutions.

Neo-classical Romanticism

Why did Romanticism come later to France? In one sense, it didn't, if we accept that Romanticism in France was an *actual social experiment*, first with the Republic, then the revolutionary wars that extended to Napoleon's imperialist adventures. The problem is that Romanticism in this sense expressed itself in the style of Neo-classicism until the 1820s. Neo-classicism, copied from ancient republican Rome, stood for a "primitive" ideal of virtue and noble simplicity against the corrupt regime of the French kings.

An example of consciously "primitive" Neo-classicism is the 1784 painting "Oath of the Horatii" by **Jacques-Louis David** (1748–1825) which anticipates the passionate republican ideals of the Revolution. Neo-classicism developed – or degenerated – into the Empire Style of the Napoleonic era, and became the suspect embodiment of the Revolution's betrayal.

Victor Hugo: Painful Rebirth

French Romanticism in another sense arose from the crushing conformism of the Restoration after Napoleon's fall. A turbulent new breed of Romantics struggled against the repression and cynical opportunism of the 1820s and succeeded in re-igniting the revolutionary fires. The voice of this generation was the poet, dramatist and novelist **Victor Hugo** (1802–85), a titanic creative force, who signalled an age of painful rebirth: "The writers of the 19th century have the good fortune of proceeding from a genesis, of arriving after an end of the world, of accompanying a reappearance of light, of being the organs of a new beginning."

*We are preceded by momentous events that impose on us the duties of **intentional reformers** and **direct civilizers**.*

Hugo reaffirmed the **past** aims of the Enlightenment but in a Romantic **present**.

Romanticism would have to confront the ideological prestige of Neo-classicism, which enshrined the "momentous events" of French history. Hugo did so in the preface to his play *Cromwell* (1827), a Romantic manifesto directed against the bygone glories of French Neo-classicism.

All systems are false; genius alone is true. . . . Let us smash theories, poetics and systems!

Shakespeare was the anti-classical model adopted by Hugo, by the novelist and playwright **Alexandre Dumas** (1802–70) and the poet and playwright **Alfred de Musset** (1810–57). These new ideas provoked serious protests. Productions of Shakespeare's plays were disrupted in Paris in 1822 and the English actors required police protection. Hugo's arch-Romantic play *Hernani* (1830), performed at the Comédie Française (spiritual home of the classical dramatist Jean Racine), sparked off a riot.

Stendhal: Romantic Realism

The novelist **Stendhal** (pseudonym of Henri Beyle, 1783–1842) was the first self-proclaimed French Romantic. His ground-breaking pamphlet *Racine and Shakespeare* (1823) defined Romanticism as a genuinely **modern** means of expression. "Modern" meant for him a disenchanted realism in sharp contrast to Hugo's revolutionary idealism. In Stendhal's view, the Romantic ego had no scope for realization in the post-Napoleonic era. Its options were reduced to a stark choice represented by the anti-hero Julien Sorel in Stendhal's early realist masterpiece *The Red and the Black* (1830).

Either the "red" of the army or the "black" of the Church . . . which will best advance me?

Julien, a carpenter's son, hypocritically chooses advancement through the Church because that seems to him the future of power in France after the Restoration of the monarchy.

Julien is a cold "premeditated" Romantic whose schemes are guided by "heroic" republican idealism and a worship of Napoleon that he is forced to keep secret. He is a dangerous force in post-revolutionary France, a "Robespierre" in disguise created by humiliation and self-repression. He seduces the wife of his employer, Madame de Rênal, in whose home he serves as tutor, to test his self-esteem in opposition to her bourgeois wealth. The novel plots the cynical rise of Julien until Mme de Rênal, still deeply in love with him, denounces him.

I despise you for the love I have made you feel – and myself for my own self-hatred.

In revenge, he shoots Mme de Rênal during Mass in their parish church. She survives the attempt, but Julien's confusion of pride, remorse and "inverted Romanticism" leads him to accept a verdict of death by guillotining. "Egotism" seems the only possible condition left to the late Romantic, as Stendhal describes in his posthumous *Memoirs of an Egotist* (1892).

Balzac: Scientist of the Novel

Honoré de Balzac (1799–1850) was another realist Romantic. He charted the entire class system of early 19th century French society in a vast series of novels collectively entitled *La Comédie humaine*. The scale of his creative enterprise is indeed "titanic", like Hugo's, but unlike him, Balzac took a dispassionate un-Romantic view of his work, seeing himself as a pathologist who categorizes, divides and subdivides the "organism" of society.

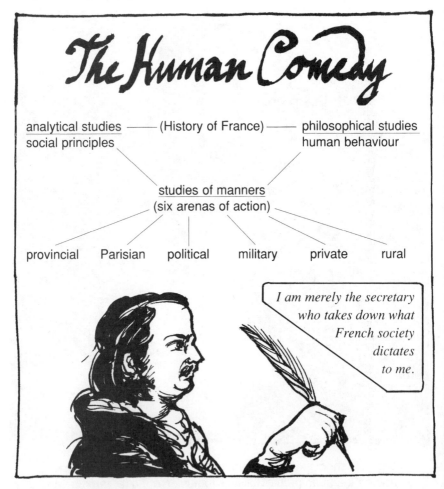

The Human Comedy

analytical studies ——— (History of France) ——— philosophical studies
social principles   human behaviour

studies of manners
(six arenas of action)

provincial   Parisian   political   military   private   rural

I am merely the secretary who takes down what French society dictates to me.

Balzac's cycle of novels can be compared to Wagner's *Ring* cycle of operas, a mythic vision of Germany, and like Wagner too he used the *Leitmotiv* of recurring characters and locations to give "organic unity" to his "human comedy".

Balzac, unlike the liberal Stendhal, was a nostalgic royalist and a political conservative. He was deeply critical of the bourgeois capitalist society emerging from nascent French industrialism, and yet fascinated by its morals. In spite of – or perhaps *because* of – his royalist conservatism, Balzac's "secretarial record" impressed Karl Marx as a unique documentary that unmasked the inner workings of capitalism.

How are fortunes made? I want to show this in its primitive stage of accumulation.

You will learn more about capitalism from Balzac than from reading a library of economic textbooks.

Balzac's cynical modern careerists part company with the archetypal Romantic searcher for "inner authenticity". But they remain close to the "daemonic" type of Faust and Don Juan in their desire for acquisition and excess. Balzac, like Stendhal, Byron and other late Romantics, is a pessimistic realist.

Early Romantic Painters

In spite of its antagonism towards the ideals of Romanticism, the Neo-classical art of Revolutionary France began to move inexorably towards Romantic forms. The artists in J.-L. David's studio were themselves among the first true Romantic painters. **A.-L. Girodet** (1767–1824) illustrated the move away from Neo-classicism with his "Ossian receiving the generals of the Republic" (1802), a combination of classical Empire Republican propaganda with newly Romantic subject matter and execution. The fictive Romantic bard is shown greeting the generals in an allegorical, fantastic setting which owes little to the ideals of David.

Either Girodet is mad or I no longer know anything of the art of painting.

Neo-classicism had one last great exponent in **J.-A.-D. Ingres** (1780–1867), but even he began to stretch the classical ideal with his sensuous surfaces and expressive distortions, and his clear fascination for the exotic, as seen in "The Great Odalisque" (1814).

I am a classical Greek . . .

The French wave of Romantic art, although delayed, was notable for the impact of Géricault and Delacroix, who brought French painting into an avantgarde position that it would maintain throughout the 19th century.

Géricault: the Romantic Apocalypse

Théodore Géricault (1791–1824) in his short but tempestuous life, like Byron, typified the Romantic artist. He introduced the energetic freedom of Constable to French Romanticism. But his own work veers to the macabre on an apocalyptic scale. His most celebrated work, "The Raft of the 'Medusa'" (1819), was based on a real event, a shipwreck tragedy, well known to viewers at the time.

I painted the separate elements from severed limbs and corpses supplied by medical students.

The absurd, gruesome plight of the castaways, driven to eat the bodies of the dead, suggested a political allegory. In 1847, the republican historian **Jules Michelet** (1798–1874) said of it: "It is France herself, our whole society, that he has embarked on this raft."

In "Liberty Leading the People" (1830), **Eugène Delacroix** (1798–1863) echoed the conditions on Géricault's raft with the victims of the 1830 Revolution who lie in the foreground of his picture. Liberty, he implies, is advancing towards us inexorably, but over the bodies of the dead – there is no possibility of gaining freedom without human suffering.

Delacroix, like Géricault, was concerned to show the drama and the counter-effect of doubt in the Romantic world-view. Like Hugo, Delacroix had a sense of the epic struggle being played out in his lifetime, and reacted not by fleeing towards the inner life, but by embracing the outer world.

I believe in the dizziness and intoxication of the creative act . . .

Orientalism

Delacroix drew inspiration from the Romantic elements in Dante, Shakespeare and Byron, but formed them into visions of emotional and sensuous immediacy which also informed his fascination with the Orient. His painting of "Greece Expiring on the Ruins of Missolonghi" (1827), produced in memory of Byron's death in the Greek War of Independence, shows a figure which is both allegorical and undeniably physical. Delacroix, despite being hailed as the leader of the Romantics, was resolutely faithful to the classical tradition.

I am purely classical . . .

The translation of the *Arabian Nights* into English in 1705–8 sparked an intense fascination with the Orient. The Orientalist **Sir William Jones** (1746–94) influenced Romantic conceptions of the East with his translations of the Hindu Vedic hymns, Persian and Arabic texts.

"The Orient" was an important mythical location in the aesthetics of the Romantic age. It was also a common setting for the Gothic novel genre. The Eastern *harem* or *seraglio* was represented as a place of abandon and wantonness where the exotic and the erotic could be freely combined for the titillation of a Western audience. This is typified in Delacroix's painting "The Death of Sardanapalus" (1827), inspired by Byron's poem of the same name.

Such violence, sensuality and amorality would have proved too shocking in a Western setting. 20th century critics have condemned Orientalism as a distorting mirror of imperialism which reflects a repressive European culture rather than anything truly Eastern.

From Republicanism to Socialism

Victor Hugo's changes of political allegiance are instructive. He accepted a post in the government of the "citizen King" Louis Philippe, who ruled in the turbulent years from the July revolution of 1830 to the revolution of 1848. Hugo's shift from conservative royalism to radical republicanism in the 1840s reflects a development of French **socialist** thinking. He was forced into exile after Napoleon III staged a *coup d'état* and declared himself Emperor (1852–70).

As a Romantic, I reject the French Revolution's Neo-classicism but embrace its republican ideals.

Hugo's early novel *Nôtre-Dame de Paris* (1831) had portrayed medieval Paris with sympathy for the poor. *Les Misérables* (1862), written from exile in the Channel Islands, was an outspoken indictment of social injustice as experienced by the hero, Jean Valjean. Hugo's portrait of the Parisian underworld is essentially "socialist".

Utopian Socialism in France: Saint-Simon

When the word "socialism" was coined in 1827 the egalitarian aims of the French Revolution were beginning to look unattainable for the labouring masses of the industrial revolution. Two figures were central to the birth of utopian socialism: Saint-Simon and Fourier.

Henri, **Comte de Saint-Simon** (1760–1825) was an aristocrat who had narrowly escaped the guillotine during the Terror. He welcomed the technological revolution as a means of redemption for mankind. By stages of "evolutionary organicism", history would culminate in a harmonious **technocracy** ruled by scientific "experts".

*Society will become a form of "workshop" in which each member functions **according to his talents**.*

This was not an egalitarian system. Although it freed women and the proletariat from oppression, the **division of labour** would still be necessary. Workers were the cogs in the machine that itself conferred a new order. Crucially, Saint-Simon's followers went on to suggest that private property was incompatible with technocracy. They also tried to set up a new "church" to enshrine Saint-Simonian ideas.

Fourier and Harmonian Man

The eccentric utopian theorist **Charles Fourier** (1772–1837) advocated the *phalanstère* or phalanx, a small-scale agricultural cooperative, as the solution to modern industrial life and the wasteful competitiveness of capitalism. Men, women and children would share in the profits. "Harmonian man" would achieve self-fulfilment through spontaneous action without the need for coercive rule. Fourier's ideas in *The Social Destiny of Man* (1808) were bizarre, yet meticulously worked out.

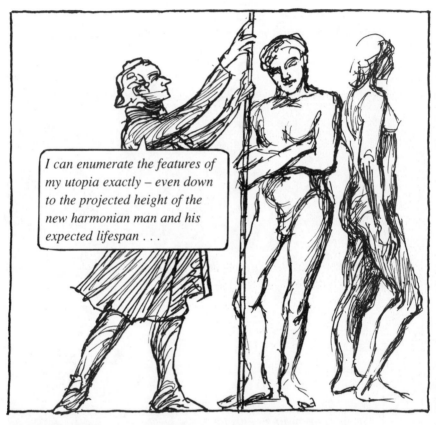

The small scale of the *phalanstère* meant that it could function within a larger framework such as a monarchy or republic. Fourier's concern with human needs and his anti-capitalism became influential during the 1848 revolution. He also had an effect on Marxian thinking. Phalanxes were actually formed in America – at Brook Farm, Massachusetts and Red Bank, New Jersey. Brook Farm members included the writer Nathaniel Hawthorne, and the commune was supported by the Transcendentalist philosopher R.W. Emerson (see pages 166, 168).

Other Socialists

Other early French socialists included **Louis-Auguste Blanqui** (1805–81), one of the first to describe himself as a communist. He favoured direct political action, with the result that he spent almost half his life in prison. Blanqui advocated insurrection by an armed élite, foreshadowing the tactics of Lenin, although Lenin's ultimate aim was the Marxist "dictatorship of the proletariat". During the street-fighting of the 1830 revolution, Blanqui is reported to have burst into the *salon* of Mlle de Montgolfier, covered in blood, shouting . . .

Louis Blanc (1811–82) pursued a less extreme, but still controversial, socialist route – the *ateliers sociaux* or national workshops, which would function independently of government. Blanc held influential beliefs on "the right to work", and like Fourier, helped set the foundations of socialist doctrine among the workers in the 1848 revolution. **Flora Tristan** (1803–44), militant feminist and pioneer syndicalist, was the first socialist to link women's emancipation and the ending of wage-slavery.

Proudhon's Anarchism

Pierre-Joseph Proudhon (1809–65) gave early French socialism an anarchistic edge. His famous work *What is Property?* (1840) argued that property is a means of exploitation. In an extreme extension of Saint-Simon's ideas, he notoriously argued . . .

Proudhon pursued the "mutualist" model in which workers would own the means of production. The implications of his work had great impact on socialist thinking in the years leading up to and beyond the 1848 revolution, in which he took an active part. His attack on poverty, exploitation and their links with property were echoed in later Marxian thinking. Proudhonian anarchism was nevertheless to develop in antagonism to Marx's doctrine of communism, an uncompromising rivalry that persisted to the Russian revolution of 1917 and well beyond to the Spanish Civil War (1936–39) and even to this day.

Karl Marx: the Last Romantic?

Karl Marx (1818–83) was not born a prophet of "capitalist doom and communist triumph". He evolved through all the embryonic stages of Romanticism first – an early interest in religion, a Byronic poet with Promethean ambitions, a Young Hegelian philosopher, a revolutionary firebrand and a campaigning journalist. Here is Marx, aged 23, characterized by a fellow German socialist, **Moses Hess** (1812–75): "Try to imagine Rousseau, Voltaire, Holbach, Lessing, Heine and Hegel combined in one person – I say *combined*, not thrown together – and you have Dr Marx."

French utopian socialism + English political economy + German idealist philosophy =

*These are what I combine in my **social science** of Communism.*

Marxism is a synthesis of these three strands of Romantic thought. But it also has roots in the Enlightenment's materialist quest for the "general laws" of society, to which the Romantic social theorists added their idea of **organic evolution**. Darwin's *The Origin of Species* (1859) is a parallel development in biology.

The Revolutions of 1848

Blanqui spoke prematurely in 1830 when he declared the "end of Romanticism". The date should be set in 1848, when the Restorationist order in Europe was shaken by revolutions in France, Italy, Austria, Hungary and Germany. In that year, Marx, with his friend **Friedrich Engels** (1820–95), published *The Communist Manifesto*, the most influential "political potboiler" of all time. The imagery Marx deploys is arch-Romantic. It begins like a Gothic thriller, with Marx a rebel Hamlet on the ramparts of Elsinore castle . . .

A spectre is haunting Europe – the spectre of Communism . . .

But the pamphlet ends with Marx's satirical massacre of Romantic utopian socialism, in his view an outmoded fantasy surpassed by bourgeois capitalism.

A Bourgeois Revolution

Marx admired bourgeois capitalism as the most advanced productive force in history so far. But it had created its own "grave-diggers" in the mass industrial working class whose final victory was assured by history. Meanwhile, however, 1848 in Marx's realist verdict was a **bourgeois** revolution, a further stage in the history of class struggles, but not yet socialist. He was right. The aims of the 1848 revolutionaries were hopelessly confused and doomed to failure.

Charles Baudelaire (1821–67) on the Paris barricades voiced his personal vendetta against his hated stepfather General Aupick. Baudelaire's poetry (*The Flowers of Evil*, 1857) signals a retreat to the inner private world of Symbolism and post-Romantic decadence. Wagner, as we have seen, forecast a dangerously racialist German nationalism. Romanticism expires on the barricades of 1848 with Marxism as its orphaned survivor.

American Romanticism

In post-rebellion America there was no extreme reformist tendency, such as Jacobinism, to introduce the kind of conspiratorial socialism that emerged in Europe. Instead, Romanticism in America took its own particular flavour from the strong legacy of 17th century dissident **Puritanism**, a severe Calvinist form of Protestantism.

A personal relationship to God – an inwardly-revealed divinity – is the only true religious experience.

Our unique sense of self supports our certainty that God intends our settlements in New England to stand as beacons for the rest of Christendom.

Taking their cue from this, and from the success of the rebellion against the British, American Romantics developed a philosophy of **individualism**, with the self as hero of its own existence, set against the backdrop of a God-given, uniquely American frontier, a modern Eden.

The Romance of the Frontier

American colonists felt a sense of sacredness in the enormity and sublimity of the landscape that God had provided for them. Proof of their "manifest destiny" came with each step in colonizing the vast continent ever further westwards. **James Fenimore Cooper** (1789–1851) idealized the self-reliance of frontier culture in historical romances like *The Last of the Mohicans* (1826). *Letters from an American Farmer* (1782) by **Jean de Crèvecoeur** (1735–1813) proposed that Americans were a distinct (if varied) race with their own robust, practical aesthetics.

Noah Webster (1758–1843) published *An American Dictionary of the English Language* in 1828, legitimizing a distinct language with simplified spellings that made more useful the ones inherited from England. This is typically Romantic – language as the sign of a "unique culture".

Hawthorne and Puritanism

In 1840, the French commentator **Alexis de Tocqueville** (1805–59) wrote that "the Americans have not yet, properly speaking, got any literature". Strangely enough, when America found its "authentic" literary voice, it was in a style of allegory and symbolism more sombre than optimistic about the American experience. **Nathaniel Hawthorne** (1804–64) explored the Puritan legacy of fundamentalist guilt, alienation and "original sin" in his great novel *The Scarlet Letter* (1850).

I do not share in the "cult of the common man" or in democratic optimism . . .

Hawthorne was unenthusiastic about the frontiersman president **Andrew Jackson** (1767–1845), and also attacked the utopian commune at Brook Farm (of which he had been a member) in *The Blithedale Romance* (1852).

The Great American Novel

Hawthorne's friend **Herman Melville** (1819–91) published his virtuoso masterpiece *Moby-Dick* in 1851. It seemed the modern epic that America had been waiting for. But it too, like Hawthorne's work and the Gothic tales of horror by **Edgar Allan Poe** (1809–49), reflected a moral ambiguity in the American soul – a conflict between pioneering free will and the "mystical blackness" of Puritan doctrine. The whaling ship *Pequod* is a "democratic" symbol of "divine equality", its crew made up of all races. Yet it is ruled by a despot, Captain Ahab, in "daemonic" quest of the white whale, Moby-Dick, the symbol of inscrutable and sublime nature.

My book is woven of ships' cables and hawsers. A Polar wind blows through it, and birds of prey hover over it.

Melville anticipates modernist techniques but is also fully Romantic in his use of melodramatic symbolism and Shakespearean sublimity.

Transcendentalism

Transcendentalism was New England's intellectual "Declaration of Independence", a native school of American mystical idealist philosophy with ideas borrowed from the English Lake School, Thomas Carlyle and German Romanticism. Its leading light was former Unitarian minister **Ralph Waldo Emerson** (1803–82), revered as a sage at his home in Concord, Massachusetts. Emerson appealed to an American way of thinking.

Why should not we have a poetry and philosophy of insight and not of tradition?

The essence of Transcendentalism is a pantheist notion of the spiritual unity in all things. This Absolute Unity, "the eternal One", can be grasped instantaneously by **intuition**. In this moment of revelation, the Transcendentalist not only sees his connection to all things, but also *contains* all variety within his own being. "I become a transparent eyeball; I am nothing; I see all; the currents of the Universal Being circulate through me; I am part or parcel of God." (Emerson)

Thoreau's Anarchism

Transcendentalism also inspired the author and pioneer ecologist **Henry David Thoreau** (1817–62), Emerson's neighbour, who lived alone in the woods at Walden Pond near Concord as an experiment in anti-materialism. Thoreau took to heart Emerson's aphorism that "Nature is the incarnation of thought. The world is the mind precipitated".

It is in vain to dream of a wildness distant from ourselves.

I shall never find in the wilds any greater wildness than I import into it.

Thoreau gave Emerson's individualism an anarchic aspect by advocating "civil disobedience" as a means of protest against government interference in the lives of individuals. This concept of libertarianism has endured well into 20th century America via the Beatniks, the hippie movement, the anti-Vietnam War protests, even the conspiratorial eco-warriors and anti-federalist "militias" currently proliferating.

Whitman: Poet of Democracy

The poet **Walt Whitman** (1819–92) was another disciple of Emerson.
Whitman, like Blake, assumed the Romantic role of prophet. He
invented a conversational, "loosened" style of "free verse" to embody
the democratic variety of "still-to-be-form'd America", as he himself
embodied it by entering into every aspect of American life in his
visionary "Protean" pilgrimages.

Whitman's single major work, *Leaves of Grass*, was constantly revised
and expanded like a diary throughout his career. A darker, elegiac
celebration of death appears beneath the surface optimism, the effect
of the traumatic and fratricidal American Civil War (1861–65) which he
experienced as a volunteer medical orderly, and the assassination of
President **Abraham Lincoln** (1809–65).

The Postmodern Romantics . . .

Romanticism is still an unfinished chapter in America. The poet **Allen Ginsberg** (1926–97) and other "on the road" Beatniks continued Whitman's mission, just as **Noam Chomsky** (b. 1928) persists in Thoreau's anarchist "civil disobedience". Examples of enduring Romanticism are easily found: an obvious one being the pioneering school of Abstract Expressionist painters seeking a "creative principle" that would prove inimitably American, with **Jackson Pollock** (1912–56) as its doomed Byron.

America is indeed a "dream", sometimes a nightmare, of endless workable contradictions – peace movements versus armed fundamentalists; democracy versus reluctant empire; wilderness versus urban decay; a place of refuge and opportunity versus dire poverty, and so on. Perhaps these are the result of America's conservative Romanticism, the invincible antagonism to socialism which is now the "manifest destiny" to which it seeks to convert the entire postmodern world. This ambition is expressed by the historian **Francis Fukuyama** (b. 1952), America's latest Romantic apologist, in *The End of History and the Last Man* (1992). Fukuyama argues in Hegelian terms that American "free market" democracy is not only a model for the world, but the **end goal** of all history.

Recurring Romanticism

Romanticism may have expired on the barricades of the 1848 revolution, but its spirit continues to haunt us. It has become common practice to see the opposition of Romanticism and classicism as a continuing dialectical process, with Western culture re-enacting the ideals and forms of each tradition in turn. If we accept this simplification, then it is possible to see the influence of Romanticism as much in the movements that reacted against it as in those that were directly inspired by it. So mid-19th century Realism can suggest as much about Romanticism through its rejection of it, as late-19th century Aestheticism or Symbolism reveal in their overt borrowings from it.

Neo-Romantic movements have resurfaced regularly. **Aestheticism**'s retreat into "art for art's sake" and **Symbolism**'s quest for occult relations between matter and spirit are recognizably Romantic, as are early-20th century German **Expressionism** with its cult of youth, ruralism and nationalist agenda, and **Surrealism** with its radical interest in the subconscious, the irrational and the macabre. American **Abstract Expressionism** is a form of therapeutic Romanticism in which the spontaneous creative *act* of painting takes precedence over "meaning".

In the arts, many of the basic tenets of Romantic aesthetics have proved extremely durable – for example, such concepts as the "organic" art form, the artist-as-genius, the "authentic" artwork, and the cult of originality which established the idea of the avantgarde and the development of art through "movements" and "influence". In recent years, deconstruction, new historicism and postmodern approaches to culture have undermined these assumptions and pointed out internal contradictions in the foundations of Romantic thinking, but the fact that we are still raising these revisionist objections shows how pervasive the Romantic influence has been. Historicist thinking in this area now debates whether we are projecting our own image onto the age and calling it "Romanticism".

The last words on this should go to Friedrich Schlegel, for whom the idea of a recurring Romanticism would have seemed quite natural. "The historian", he said, "is a prophet turned backward".

Perhaps a new Romanticism will provide us with a way out of the impasse of postmodernism.

Further Reading

Background to Romanticism
Frederick C. Beiser, *Enlightenment, Revolution, and Romanticism* (Cambridge MA: Harvard University Press, 1992)
Isaiah Berlin, *Roots of Romanticism* (London and New York: Vintage, 1999)

General studies of Romanticism
Aidan Day, *Romanticism* (London and New York: Routledge, 1995)
Hugh Honour, *Romanticism* (1979; London: Pelican, 1981)
Arthur O. Lovejoy, "On the Discrimination of Romanticisms" (1924), in *Essays in the History of Ideas* (New York: Puttnam, 1960)

Philosophical links
Jacques Barzun, *Classic, Romantic, and Modern* (1961; Chicago: University of Chicago Press, 1975)
Russell B. Goodman, *American Philosophy and the Romantic Tradition* (Cambridge: Cambridge University Press, 1991)
Mark Kipperman, *Beyond Enchantment: German Idealism and English Romantic Poetry* (Philadelphia: University of Pennsylvania Press, 1986)
Philippe Lacoue-Labarthe, Jean-Luc Nancy (trans. P. Barnard, C. Lester), *The Literary Absolute* (Albany: State University of New York Press, 1988)

Literary criticism
M.H. Abrams, *The Mirror and the Lamp: Romantic Theory and the Critical Tradition* (Oxford and New York: Oxford University Press, 1953)
M.H. Abrams (ed.), *English Romantic Poets: Modern Essays in Criticism* (New York: Oxford University Press, 1960)
Jonathan Bate (ed.), *The Romantics on Shakespeare* (Harmondsworth: Penguin, 1992)
Harold Bloom (ed.), *Romanticism and Consciousness: Essays in Criticism* (New York: Norton, 1970)
Harold Bloom, *The Anxiety of Influence: A Theory of Poetry* (London and New York: Oxford University Press, 1973)
Andrew Bowie, *From Romanticism to Critical Theory* (London and New York: Routledge, 1996)
David Bromwich (ed.), *Romantic Critical Essays* (Cambridge: Cambridge University Press, 1987)
Paul de Man, *The Rhetoric of Romanticism* (New York: Columbia University Press, 1984)
Jerome J. McGann, *The Romantic Ideology: A Critical Investigation* (Chicago and London: University of Chicago Press, 1983)
Duncan Wu, *Romanticism: A Critical Reader* (Oxford and Cambridge MA: Blackwell, 1995)

Music
Alfred Einstein, *Music in the Romantic Era* (New York: Norton, 1947)

Visual arts
William Vaughan, *Romanticism and Art* (London: Thames and Hudson 1994)
William Vaughan, *The Romantic Spirit in German Art 1790–1990* (London: Thames and Hudson 1994)

Women's studies
Meena Alexander, *Women in Romanticism* (London: Macmillan, 1989)
Margaret Homans, *Bearing the Word. Language and Female Experience in Nineteenth-Century Women's Writing* (Chicago: University of Chicago Press, 1986)
Anne K. Mellor (ed.), *Romanticism and Feminism* (Bloomington: Indiana University Press, 1988)

Political, historical and cultural contexts
Marilyn Butler, *Romantics, Rebels and Reactionaries: English Literature and its Background 1760–1830* (Oxford: Oxford University Press, 1981)
Eric Hobsbawm, *The Age of Revolution, 1789–1848* (London: Weidenfeld and Nicolson, 1975)
Simon Schama, *Landscape and Memory* (London: HarperCollins 1995)
David Simpson, *Romanticism, Nationalism and the Revolt Against Theory* (London and New York: Routledge, 1992)
E.P. Thompson, *The Making of the English Working Class* (1963; Harmondsworth: Penguin, 1991)
Raymond Williams, *Culture and Society 1780–1850* (1958; New York: Columbia University Press, 1983)

Author's Acknowledgements

I am particularly indebted to Richard Appignanesi for his inspired editing, and I would also like to thank the following for their advice and encouragement: Toby Clark, Simon Flynn, Ann Harrison-Broninski, Alison Heath, Chris Horrocks, Róisín Leggett and Michael Venman.

I would like to dedicate this book to my father, and to the memory of my mother.

Artist's Acknowledgements

Many thanks to Richard Appignanesi and Duncan Heath, Ed Bright, Simon Flynn, Mick Gowar, Gaye Lockwood, Pam Smy and especially Martin Salisbury for all their help and support.

Typesetting by **Wayzgoose**

Duncan Heath studied English Literature at Oxford University, and now works as a writer and editor for a publishing company.

Judy Boreham recently graduated from the Royal College of Art, and is working as a freelance illustrator in Cambridge.

Index